PRAISE FOR YOU DIDN'T COMPLETE ME
BY JOANNA HARRIS

This book is long over-due. JoAnna's witty and candid presentation of her own first-hand encounter with heartache will provide many young women with the encouragement needed to turn the corner and breathe again. This one little book contains more insight than countless therapy sessions at 90 bucks an hour. Do the math—buy the book!

—Vicki Courtney, National speaker and Author of
The Virtuous Woman: Shattering the Superwoman Myth

This book is uplifting as well as entertaining. JoAnna speaks from the heart. She shares her fears, sorrow and how she experienced life by overcoming her biggest fear—the loss of love. This book is wonderful for all ages and should be shared with your girlfriends.

—Heather, 30, Ohio

With humor similar to David Sedaris, Joanna's stream-of-conscious style is perfect delivery for these deep issues so many women face today. I could completely relate to her thought process and the hope she eventually discovered in God through her heartbreaks. Every 20-30 something woman should read this book.

—Elizabeth, 28-year-old wife and mother, Florida

Hysterical! Charming! JoAnna hits right at the heart of every woman. Thank the Lord for her heartaches—where would we be without them? She leaves us screaming, "WE WANT MORE!!!" If you've ever been in love or even thought about it, then this book's for you!

—Anna, 27, Mississippi

Joanna's bravery, honesty, and ability to look at tough situations with a sense of humor is what makes her book so wonderful. It is a must-read for any girl who has the intentions of getting married one day.

—Kirstin, 21, Ohio

Wow! JoAnna captures one of life's most sensitive and painful moments with humor, honesty, vulnerability, and triumph. This is a must-read for all who dare to love.

—Jennifer, 28, Tennessee

This is going to be a book I read over and over and recommend to all my friends. I laughed out loud, I highlighted like crazy, and most of all, I felt that warm, fuzzy feeling you get when you're reminded of how good God is and how much he loves you. JoAnna has crafted a jewel of a book – funny, touching, thought provoking . . . but most of all, filled with truth from God's word. I loved every single page!

—Joni

JoAnna's wit, combined with her honest writing, is a real blessing. God has truly gifted her with the ability to communicate her life experiences effectively and captivate her audience from beginning to end. You've got to read this.

—Brooke

I loved JoAnna Harris' book. This is would be a great book for someone that went through a heartbreak five days ago, five months ago, or even five years ago! Awesome!

—Christy

JoAnna Harris is the greatest author of our time.

—JoAnna's Mom

JoAnna's brutal honesty about relationships relates to the reader in a way that most books don't. A definite must-read.

—Tonia, 26, Georgia

You **Didn't** Complete Me

You **Didn't** Complete Me

When "The One" Turns Out to Be Just "Someone"

JoAnna Harris

W PUBLISHING GROUP
A Division of Thomas Nelson Publishers
Since 1798

www.wpublishinggroup.com

YOU DIDN'T COMPLETE ME

© 2004 JoAnna Harris.

Published by W Publishing Group, a Division of Thomas Nelson, Inc., P.O. Box 141000, Nashville, Tennessee 37214.

All Scripture quotations, unless otherwise indicated, are taken from *The Holy Bible, New International Version* (NIV). Copyright © 1973, 1978, 1984, International Bible Society. Used by permission of Zondervan Bible Publishers.

Other Scripture references are from the following source: *The Message* (MSG), copyright © 1993. Used by permission of NavPress Publishing Group.

Editorial Staff: Lori Jones, Deborah Wiseman, Ramona Richards
Cover Design: Matt Lehman for Anderson Thomas Design, Nashville, Tennessee
Page Design: Lindsay Carreker for Book & Graphic Design, Nashville, Tennessee

Library of Congress Cataloging-in-Publication Data

Harris, JoAnna, 1974–
    You didn't complete me : when "the one" turns out to be just "someone" / JoAnna Harris.
      p. cm.
    ISBN 0-8499-4525-9
    1. Harris, JoAnna, 1974– 2. Man-woman relationships. I. Title.
CT275.H3858A3 2004
306.7'02'07—dc22

                           2004013876

Printed in the United States of America

04 05 06 07 08 PHX 9 8 7 6 5 4 3 2

In lieu of Prozac, I wrote this book.
May it have the same effect for you.

CONTENTS

Contents

AUTHOR'S **NOTE**

Have you had a recent heart trauma? Did your relationship end abruptly? Are you confused and dazed and maybe a little ticked off? Don't worry. I'm not going to say things like "This too shall pass" (even though it will) or "This will only make you stronger" (even though it could) or "You're better off without him" (even though you might be). I won't say these things because I know that right now they are just words, and sometimes words can do nothing to reach the hurt. I remember people saying these exact things to me immediately after my big breakup. It made me want to punch them squarely in the face and scream that they had no idea how I was feeling. But that would have been rash. Some of the advice-givers were sincere and genuinely cared for me. And some were just nosy. I promise to not be nosy. I won't pretend to know your hurt or your situation. I promise to not offer empty advice or any lame how-to's on getting over him. Breaking up stinks. I know. Far. Too. Well. So in light of that, I'll just try to be honest about myself and all that has happened and all that is happening in my life. And I'll hope that you too can find rest.

P.S. Appropriate names, dates, and states have been altered to protect the guilty parties involved in this true account of a harrowing heartache.

INTRODUCTION

Breaking Up: Surviving the First Ten Days

Day One: Do not get out of bed. At all. It's best to not even open your eyes. Do not call him.

Day Two: Open eyes and maybe get up to get some water to drink. Other than that, stay in bed. Call best friend and ask her to come over and hide all romantic comedies and sappy dramas and place all pictures of The Ex in a box to be used later. Do not call him.

Day Three: Turn on TV and channel-surf while wondering about the meaning of life. Shout at the happy couples in TV commercials and sitcoms. Anytime a male character tells a female character something sweet or thoughtful, scream "LIAR!" as loud as you can. Call best friend and ask her to make you a Breakup Alert Bracelet that will flash a warning when anyone asks you about your former significant other. Do not call him.

Day Four: Move your bed into the living room so you can watch the big TV and continue shouting. This also gives better access to the freezer that your best friend has wisely stocked with ice cream in easy-to-eat-in-one-sitting pints. Begin eating. Do not keep count. Do not call him.

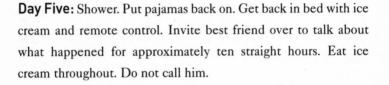

Day Five: Shower. Put pajamas back on. Get back in bed with ice cream and remote control. Invite best friend over to talk about what happened for approximately ten straight hours. Eat ice cream throughout. Do not call him.

Day Six: Go to drugstore. Do not listen to radio on the way to drugstore for fear of hearing "your song." Buy more ice cream, Kleenex, and lotion with aloe since using paper towels to blow nose has caused severe chaffing. While there, also buy the latest celebrity gossip magazines. Go home and read magazines while considering the complexities of love. Even the rich and beautiful get dumped. Do not call him.

Day Seven: Finally return the eighty-five voice mails from your mother. Assure her that you are fine. Attempt to sound light and breezy—cheery even. Tell her that breaking up was the best thing for both of you, and you are happy about it. Hang up and cry. Eat more ice cream. Do not call him.

Day Eight: Craft Day. Find scissors and go through box of pictures. To try: Cut out The Ex's head in every picture and replace with pictures of Brad Pitt or Orlando Bloom. Cut all pictures of him into tiny confetti pieces (best if done near New Year's). Take all letters and cards from him and cut out words of sentiment and love. Make refrigerator magnets out of these words and tell your friends, "These are lies that boys tell." Do not call him.

Day Nine: Begin to reenter society. Shower again and put on real clothes. Meet two or three close girlfriends for dinner—preferably at a Mexican restaurant to lessen chances of hearing "your song" played overhead. If a random acquaintance sees you and asks about The Ex, flash your Breakup Alert Bracelet and shoo them away. Do not call him.

Day Ten: Go back to work. Wear short sleeves so that your Breakup Alert Bracelet is in plain view to any well-wishers who want to offer lame advice and hurtful clichés that mean nothing. Do not call him.

CHAPTER **ONE**

Red Socks: How I Met My Match

I don't really know how to write down the biggest heartbreaks of my life. I suppose if I do it I will be called brave or courageous. But I'm not. It's hard to talk about them even now, spilling all my secrets. It's hard to tell the story. What once was a dream come true now seems too horrid to describe. Like a joke. Not a funny ha-ha joke, but a cruel one intended for evil or to embarrass me. And that's how I feel about it now. Red-faced with sweaty palms. An overwhelming urge to run and run until I arrive somewhere where no one knows the story. Where no one knows that I've now had my heart smashed into tiny little pieces—twice. And yet, here I am, telling the story for all to see. What's my motivation? Cheap therapy, I suppose.

Maybe I'll start out by telling a little about myself. I love to watch TV and drink way too much Diet Coke. I have a lifelong love affair with French fries. I love to read really good books and subscribe to far too many magazines. I tend to be cliquish accidentally, which causes people to think I'm snobby. I'm a world champion Nertz card game player—at least among my friends. I'm more spicy than sweet, with food and with life. Lately, I've become an avid treadmill runner and I'm turning thirty this year. Oh yeah, and my fiancé broke up with me two months before our wedding date. That about sums me up.

Isn't it funny that the sentences that affect us most are typically the shortest? *You got the job. You're fired. I met someone else. I'm pregnant. There's been an accident. We won! We lost. Wanna go out sometime? Will you marry me? We need to talk. I love you. I hate you.* And the best one, of course—*I have to tell you something.* Nothing good ever comes from someone saying they have to tell you something. Good news tends to burst right out. Bad news usually needs a setup. A short sentence that recently changed my life's direction was *I think it's too soon.* Meaning: *I think it's too soon for us to proceed with our wedding in two months.* This coming from the man who had asked me to marry him months earlier. I had a ring and everything—the dress, the church, the bridesmaids, the flowers, the invitations, the food, the musicians—and he changed his mind. I guess he got scared. I still don't really know.

> I remember everything about him and me and the room and the temperature and his face. But I still don't know how it happened.

I remember everything about him and me and the room and the temperature and his face. But I still don't know how it happened. He just said it. And I knew it would change my life. We were sitting on opposite ends of the couch in his apartment when he said it. His expression made me feel that if I made any sudden movements he would scurry away. I wanted to lunge at him. Beg him to not do this. Command him to snap out of it. Find out where he was and demand that this impostor in front of me bring back the real Ross. I wanted to be an action movie star and jump on my motorcycle and ride to freedom, never looking back. I wanted to fly backward around the world like Superman and turn back time. I wanted to say all the right things, but all I could manage was good-bye.

After that I sort of just numbly existed for a while. Everyone kept asking how I was doing, and I never could fully answer them because I didn't fully know. I should have been prepared, I guess. This wasn't the first time my heart had been ripped apart in front of my very eyes, so my friends were concerned I might lose it this time (I came pretty close to the edge the first time around). I was a roller coaster of emotions—and not the kiddie kind that just goes around in a circle with the occasional slight hill that makes you giggle. I was the kind that has thirteen warning signs on the way to it and three different safety harnesses once you get to it and then a place to vomit after you finally get off it. I had good days and okay days and very dark days. I had really hilarious moments and moments when I thought I would collapse if one more person asked me how I was doing in their best "bless your heart" tone of voice. (I really hate that tone.)

And it was everyone, even people I mildly knew. I was tossed all day between those who felt sorry for me and those who thought it was about time I cheered up. Every expectation from every person was different. Even the expectations I put on myself were different. Everyone said I should be true to my feelings—be true to myself. Little did they know that inside, my true self was a raging parallel. I was glad he was out of my life. I missed him desperately. I was angry. I was sad. I was content. I was misplaced. I wished that things had gone as planned and that I was still getting married. I was relieved that I wasn't getting married. I was back where I belonged. I didn't belong anywhere. I felt guilty. I felt free. I felt strong and liberated. I felt like I would crumble at any moment.

It was hard. Hard to be myself when I didn't know who that was at the moment. Hard to live up to my old reputation when everything had changed so suddenly. Hard to fake it. Hard to be real. I was constantly overwhelmed with the feeling that I wanted to run. Physically and mentally and emotionally I wanted to run. To hide out. I wanted to go somewhere where no one knew me—where there wasn't any "way it used to be." But I knew I would long to be among my friends if I wasn't. I knew I would regret the run. Regret the chance to get my life back. To change it. To make it better somehow.

Everyone said Ross must have gone crazy. Must not have been God's will for my life. Said things like, "Yup, men . . . they never change." Funny, these exact people had, moments earlier, said things like, "It's so obvious that he's The One. It's so great to see two people so meant for each other." Hmm. When we were together and Ross would say or do nice things, doubters told me to beware because people change. Then when he broke my heart, these same doubters pointed out that people don't change. Well, which is it? I'd like to know. Because I'm starting to get the feeling that no one knows. That there is no formula or exact science for love or even for life. No one knows what will or will not happen. No one knows how other people will react in certain situations—they don't really even know how they will react themselves. But it seems to be the cool thing to act like you know. Everyone has advice and wisdom and words. Lots and lots of words.

I needed someone to blame. I wanted to know whose fault it was. Was it mine? His? All the nosy naysayers? It's worse when there's no one to blame. I mean, I could blame Ross. I could point all ten fingers at him and vilify him as if he were an evil monster. (And for a while I did.) But the truth is that it just didn't work. We weren't in the same place at the same time, emotionally speaking. He got scared and ran. I didn't try to catch up.

Then there was the matter of God's role in this whole mess. When things were good, happy, everyone thought it was God's will! Yea rah for love! God is good! Then when things fell apart it was apparent to everyone (except me) that I was clearly out of God's will for my life. After all, he was a "nice, Christian guy," right? I was told that I should do some serious praying and Bible reading and get back on track. When things with Ross were good, I guess everyone assumed that my relationship with God was A-OK, since I found The One and all. Then when it ended, the assumption was that my relationship with God must be in shambles. Umm . . . what?

It doesn't help when people constantly speak into your hurt like they belong there. Like they know. Like they have any idea. It was hard enough to take a shower and leave the house. I didn't need random people telling me that God must be mad at me for this to have happened. That I must have unconfessed sin in my black heart. That I must have made the wrong choice. That it must be me and something I did wrong.

I remember first hearing about Ross from my friend AJ. AJ worked with me and lived with me and traveled with me and made me laugh. She had recently met someone new and had just gotten back from visiting him at his home—in Boston of all places. I was quite supportive of her starting a long-distance relationship and told her that it would work out if it was meant to be. Assured her that all the bad rumors about long-distance relationships weren't necessarily true. AJ was in my office telling me about her trip and her new guy, Steve—and New Guy Steve's roommate, Ross. She said, in fact, that New Guy Steve's roommate, Ross, would be an absolutely perfect new guy for me. Uh-uh. No way. I was not interested in a long-distance relationship. Sure, it was okay for her and all the rest of the world. Just not me. I was too busy. Too fine with the way things were. Too content. I'd already had enough heartbreak for two lifetimes. Maybe three. And I wasn't interested in dating anyone, let alone someone in Boston.

So AJ told me all about Roommate Ross and how he was so cute and so funny and so everything I needed in a man. I nodded and "Mmm-hmmd" and thought little of it. A few weeks went by and AJ was still talking up Roommate Ross. One night AJ and I were having dinner and she was telling me how Roommate Ross was a huge Boston Red Sox fan. I laughed and said, Wouldn't it be hilarious if I sent him an actual pair of red socks? AJ screamed, YES! and DO IT!! I thought why not? He lived in Boston after all. It wasn't like it mattered.

AJ and I went to Wal-Mart that very night and I bought a pair of red socks. Then I wrote a poem about red socks and mailed the poem, with the socks, to Roommate Ross in Boston. The poem read:

> *I'm sending a pair of red socks*
> *I'm sending these socks in a box*
> *I hope you don't care*
> *I sent you this pair*
> *But it's fun sending socks to a fox.*

I sent this poem to a guy I had never met or spoken to or communicated with on any level. It's not something I've ever done before. I think AJ also might have made some joke about Roommate Ross being the potential love of my life, which cracked us both up. The Red Socks package wasn't an attempt to catch a man. Or to even lure a man. It was a dare, mostly, and something funny to do. It made me laugh. That was pretty much it.

About a week later I got an e-mail from Roommate Ross thanking me for the socks and the poem and telling me a bit about himself. Apparently Steve had simultaneously been talking me up as Roommate JoAnna, so Roommate Ross knew who I was. In his e-mail he told me things like what kind of music he liked and what kind of car he drove. He told me what sports teams were his favorites and that he wasn't sure why he was e-mailing a strange girl in Nashville. His e-mail was funny and intriguing and surprising. So I e-mailed him back.

It's interesting to me how relationships start. Especially the big ones. The ones that change your life and your perspective. The ones people write songs about. (And books.) My parents met at church. Mom had been a churchgoer her whole life and Dad was just starting out. While at college in Bowling Green, Kentucky, a friend asked Dad to come to a college thing at his church. Dad wasn't interested until he learned that there would be girls there. Lots of girls. So he went to check it out.

Story goes that Mom saw him, went over and asked to share his hymnal. Halfway through the song Dad noticed that Mom knew all the words. They've been married now for thirty-three years. I think sometimes we expect relationships to start like they do in the movies—and sometimes they do. My parents are evidence of that. I know someone who really did meet her husband in the produce section of a grocery store. He noticed her among the grapes and bananas and stopped her in the parking lot to ask her out. Long ago, my granny was riding past my papa's house on her bicycle. Papa said to his mother, "You see that little girl? I'm gonna marry her." She quickly responded, "You better leave that girl alone!" Forty-six years and four sons later, turns out my papa was right about that little girl.

People often say love happens when you aren't looking for it to happen. I think this concept is comical because it causes people to "look" while appearing to be disinterested. If a person is aware of the looking process, then they are looking. In fact, I'll go so far as to say that I don't know anyone who is single and not looking on some level. Not one person.

We all listen to one another's stories and secretly plot, Maybe that will work for me! I guess I should ask a handsome stranger if I can share his hymnal. But my church doesn't use hymnals, so I guess I'm doomed to never meet The One. I personally like the stories of couples who didn't like each other at first. Especially if only one person is interested and the other is most definitely not. I like the chase scene with a happy ending. I like the story. I like the idea. Because the beginnings of relationships are the best part. (Well, to me the beginnings are the best part. All of my relationships have ended at some time or another, so I tend to like beginnings.) I like being nervous and wondering what he thinks.

I like secret smiles and casual flirting that is indeed calculated and pored over with girlfriends during late-night discussions. I like acting disinterested even though I'm so very interested I might swoon. It's fun. This should not be misconstrued as playing mind games or relationship games or whatever that is. I'm just talking about the chemistry of the flirt. The hair toss. The laugh. The eye twinkle. When every slight nuance has meaning and hope. When he laughs at my joke and I feel certain he thinks I'm the funniest woman he's ever known. This process can also backfire when he talks about another girl and how funny she is. This will either cause me to give up all hope or to casually flirt even more casually. But it's all part of the beginning. It's all fun. Scary and frustrating and oh-so-fun.

> I tend to have multiple personalities when it comes to meeting a new guy.

Of course, beginnings can also be quite disturbing. I tend to have multiple personalities when it comes to meeting a new guy. I don't know why this is—and no, I have never sought medical help. I've come to accept it and sometimes I kinda like it. Besides, shouldn't The One find my diverse persona charming and delightful? I think so.

When it comes to meeting cute boys, I have ten, maybe twelve different personalities. First, there's Chatty Girl. Chatty Girl gets nervous around cute boys and fills the awkwardness by talking about anything and everything and never shutting up ever because she's afraid that any silence will surely be bad so she should talk and talk and talk. She doesn't always know what she's talking about and seldom ever cares what she's talking about. She just needs to talk so that she won't feel weird and embarrassed. This will either make Cute Boy laugh or want to gouge his eyes out with hot irons.

Sometimes I'm Giggly Girl. Giggly Girl is so annoying, even to me. She just giggles—incessantly. Everything is hilariously hilarious and Giggly Girl has no control. She tears up because she giggles so hard. She has body convulsions with no sound. She bends over and slaps her knee and inhales deeply and then starts all over again. Giggly Girl gets on my nerves.

I kinda like Shy Girl. Shy Girl is bashful and sweet and quiet. This can be interpreted by Cute Boy as being a good listener or low maintenance, neither of which is true. If the boy is really super cute, Shy Girl will come out. She'll laugh slightly and maintain a modest smile at all times. She says little, but it can't last long.

It can't last long because there's Crazy Girl. Crazy Girl is my dominant personality. She's loud and obnoxious and the life of the party. She likes to laugh loudly and contribute to every conversation in the room. Her jokes are usually clever and funny, but there tends to be too many of them. Crazy Girl has a good time all the time. Sometimes Cute Boy will be drawn to Crazy Girl's good-time fun. But he's usually just as quickly aggravated and apt to leave. Bye-bye, Cute Boy. That's what Crazy Girl says.

My other dominant personality is Mean Sarcastic Girl. I do like her, but I can see why she's not the best representation of me when meeting someone new—and cute. Mean Sarcastic Girl thinks she should take every jab available to her, be it about Cute Boy or anyone else. She thinks she's so funny and clever. She makes fun of Cute Boy even though she likes him. She makes herself appear superior to Cute Boy with wry comments that she doesn't really mean. Sometimes she says, "Just joking," and thinks that will make it all okay. But it doesn't. Cute Boy just thinks she's mean. Mean Sarcastic Girl is twins with Smart Girl. Smart Girl thinks she's sooo smart. Cute Boy doesn't like her either.

I tend to favor Flirty Busy Girl. Flirty Busy Girl giggles, but not too much, and flips her hair and has a twinkle in her eye. Flirty Busy Girl will touch Cute Boy on the arm when she talks to him, but only absent-mindedly. Flirty Busy Girl will flirt just enough to get Cute Boy interested and then she'll have other plans. She's flirty. She's busy. She drives Cute Boy wild.

Then there's Self-Conscious Girl, whom I tend to feel sorry for. If Cute Boy tells her she looks cute, she is puzzled and runs to the bathroom to look in the mirror and figure out why he said such a thing. Was she not cute yesterday? What about her is cute today? Why would he say that? Is he just joking with her? Is he secretly laughing at her? What does it all mean!

Athletic Girl thinks all boys want an athletic girl so she talks about working out and watching sports—but only in front of Cute Boy. The rest of the time she would rather shop and watch romantic comedies and eat ice cream.

Bossy Self-Centered Girl is . . . well . . . bossy and self-centered. Cute Boy is allowed to take her to only the restaurants that she likes. Cute Boy is allowed to watch only movies that she likes to watch. Cute Boy must give Bossy Self-Centered Girl the remote. This is in the best interest of Cute Boy because if he does not comply, Monster Girl may show up.

And the worst of all is Monster Girl because you never know when she might appear. But when she does—look out—her eyes will flash red and her fangs will come out and she just might claw Cute Boy to death. If Cute Boy makes some comment that Monster Girl doesn't like or disagrees with, she will scream and become enraged.

This always happens suddenly and without warning. Like the other day when a cute boy drove me to lunch. I started out as Shy Girl and tried to make conversation about a record I had recently bought. Cute Boy made a comment about the record that I didn't like, and I hit him in the arm and yelled at him that he was wrong, wrong, wrong. Hi, Monster Girl. Cute Boy just laughed and turned up the radio—but it was a song I didn't like. Bossy Self-Centered Girl suddenly emerged and forcefully urged him to turn it down that instant. He didn't. He didn't seem to care that there were three girls all riding in his front seat.

No wonder boys break up with me. They may meet me as Shy Girl and end up with Crazy Girl. It's enough to make any sane man run.

My beginning with Ross was different from most, given our respective locations. Our beginning was played out in words. We e-mailed and we talked. We flirted and revealed. He didn't really get the chance to see all of my personalities. (How unfortunate for him!) It was easier to be honest and easier to hide things. Easier to be confident and easier to be exactly whom I had always wanted to be. And I liked him in an instant. Our pasts were very similar. My father is a Baptist preacher and his is too. I grew up attending a Christian school and so did he. I can quote the movie *Tombstone* and he can too (only he does the voices better). We wanted the same things in life. Had the same ideals. The same outlook. Early on in the e-mail exchange we began making lists. Lists of funny things and quirky things and important things. I found him interesting, witty, intriguing, and fascinating. I wanted to know more.

We e-mailed every day for a week. That weekend I went to my cousin's wedding in Kentucky and had all manner of relatives ask me if I was ever going to get married. They asked in hushed tones with shifty eyes, like they thought I wouldn't want anyone to know that I was . . . inhale deeply . . . not married yet. It made me mad and it made me think about Ross in Boston. So far, his e-mails had been the highlight of my days. Yeah, it had only been a week. But a good week. A bright week. I drove back from the wedding and went to a birthday party for my boss's daughter, Parker. She was turning two. Everyone at the party was married and had children. Many children. Multitudes of children. This made my ovaries anxious so I left early. I went to the office—late on a Saturday night—and e-mailed Ross in Boston, knowing that I was either very very pathetic or very very smitten. I took it as the first sign that this no-big-deal thing with Roommate Ross might be going somewhere. That it might be more than a joke or just kidding around. That I might really like this guy. After one week and seven e-mails.

That's sort of my track record. I tend to leap into like (or love). The expression *falling in love* doesn't adequately describe my actions. I don't accidentally fall—I run and jump. I scream Wheee!!! It's just my nature. This can be very fun—and can also lead to a painful crash on the jagged rocks below. Maybe that's why others *fall* instead of *leap*. Maybe they are wary of the rocks. The danger. The peril. Not me—I think about the jump. The free fall. The fun. Either way—falling or leaping—the landing can sometimes be bad. Even worse when the leaper is not prepared for what's below. But I'm skipping ahead of myself.

CHAPTER **TWO**

The Story

I will now attempt to recount, as best I can, what happened next.

For two months Ross and I talked on the phone incessantly and sent flirty e-mails and love letters and cards. We talked about everything—the big issues and favorite movies and life dreams and Coke-or-Pepsi. We talked about children and what we would name them and weddings and what kind ours would be. After two months I met his family and he met mine. And every step of the way I loved him more.

I found him to be kind and giving and responsible and fun. He loved Jesus and wanted to love Him more. And he loved me. Things between us were easy and natural. We had amazing chemistry together. To me, all that added up to mean forever. Some thought it was impossible to be sure since we had known each other for only a few months. (Five, to be exact.) But we knew. Through and through. I explained to the doubters that love isn't an equation with exact parameters. It's just love. I didn't choose to love Ross. Didn't calculate if this was the right time of my life or if he was my mathematical match. I just loved him. He just loved me. We had both found our hearts' happiness.

> Wasn't abandoning all for love what life was about?

Ross and I decided that I would move to Boston at Christmas, two months before the wedding. He could stay at his parents' during that time and I could live in his (our future) apartment and we could see each other every day. Bliss! It seemed like the logical decision, easy enough. Except that I would have to quit my job, leave my family, leave my church, leave all of my friends, leave the South where I had always always lived, and move to the North, where I knew nothing about the way things worked. But, it was for love. For forever. It was worth it to me. Ross was the single most important person in my life, and I would make any sacrifice necessary for him.

Some of my friends voiced (rather loudly) that they felt I was making all the sacrifices and he wasn't making any. Even when I would try to explain those accusations away, I felt there might be some truth to what they were saying. But over and over I argued that love was worth the risk. Wasn't abandoning all for love what life was about? Weren't there scores of songs about love being the ultimate? The one goal in life? Who cares about sacrifice when you've got love?!

And I did love him. Everything about him. His laugh and his heart and his faith and his drive and his hands and his family. His outlook and his sensitivity and his sense of responsibility and his intellect and his face and his patience and his character. Even more. There wasn't a moment when I doubted my love for him. There were times I got nervous about logistics and my own personal demons of self-doubt and my insatiable desire to control my life. But all in all I was sure. Ready. Delighted, even. This was my moment. My time!

The plan was for Ross to fly in on December 23 and spend Christmas with my family and then we would drive to Boston. I had previously sent up most of my belongings by way of a friend and a truck. The rest I'd cram into my Honda, say good-bye to my friends—and my life—and go to the airport to get Ross. To start my new life. To push the big green button that says, *This is it—no turning back!* But leaving my life is harder than I was prepared for. I feel euphoric and depressed all at once. But I try to concentrate on what is ahead. Love and marriage. Ross.

I park the car at the airport and go in to meet him, feeling happier than I think I've ever felt before. Or maybe a different kind of happy. New Happy. I see him through the crowd and run to greet him—and his embrace seems forced. I stand back to look at him and hush away any thoughts of forced embraces. We go down to baggage claim and the forced-ness becomes worse. I sense him move, ever so slightly, away from me as I move closer. It isn't a move anyone else would notice, but I feel as if he is screaming and running away. I ask him if he is okay, and he says he thinks he may have eaten some bad pizza at his layover in Cincinnati. Good, I think. Nothing serious . . . just some pizza. All is well. By the time we load the luggage and fight through traffic to reach the interstate, I feel uneasy. I turn and ask Ross if he is happy to see me. He says, Yeah. For some reason, I don't believe him.

Christmas is a welcome whirlwind that leaves little time to think about the weird vibe between us. The forced embrace. The new look on his face. It's all relatives and dinners and presents and Christmas. Then, at 6 AM on the day after Christmas, we begin the drive 1,296 miles north. It begins to set in for me that something is amiss. Off kilter. I drive first and Ross sleeps some. which gives me lots of time to think. Most of that time is spent trying to rationalize myself out of a panic. Trying to convince myself that I have an overly active imagination and I am probably making something out of nothing. That it isn't remotely possible that something is wrong between us. We are perfect together. He adores me. We are getting married. I look at the diamond in my engagement ring as it shines in the sunlight. This is reality. Shiny happiness. Whatever crazy thoughts I am deriving from a few strange comments are simply products of a long trip and working too much. (He had been working nonstop so that we could spend more time together when I got to Boston.) Ross is fine. Tired and overworked, but fine. And I am fine. We are fine.

In about the eighth hour of driving we are both silent and I am thinking about my life and how with each second it changes dramatically as we drive north. About how I'm on the verge of marrying this person next to me. About how we should just clear up whatever it is that's looming over both our heads. Even though I feel sure it's nothing, it's probably best to address it calmly and find the solution and move on. I look over at him and smile. I joke lightheartedly that he can't break up with me now because I just left my job and my house and my friends and my family—and I would have nowhere to go. But he doesn't laugh at my little joke. I suddenly feel as if oxygen masks have dropped from the ceiling and we are spiraling toward our fiery deaths. Until this moment we have never had one argument or disagreement. This situation, however, is neither an argument nor a disagreement. It's something much worse.

Twenty-two hours from the time we leave my parents' house we arrive in Boston deliriously tired. I walk into his apartment and immediately lie down on the couch and fall into a profoundly deep sleep. An anesthetic kind of dream sleep that seems to go by in a blink. Hours later I wake up and find a note from Ross saying that he's gone into work and will be back later, right as he walks in the door. I feel displaced and confused, still in a fog from sleep. We drove for twenty-two hours straight and he decided to go to work? He suggests that we go to the grocery store so I can have some food in the house, and off we go. We suddenly realize how ravenous we are, so we stop at Subway, and while we're eating I ask him what kinds of things I should buy to make for dinner that week. (Because I don't have a job and my one daily task will be to make dinner for Ross.) He just glares at me. (He had never glared before, ever.) I go on to say that I can make dinner every night and we can spend some time together. Ross shifts uncomfortably in his seat and looks everywhere but at me. He says he doesn't know if he'll be able to make dinner every night. He says that he will have to work late sometimes and will want to get a pizza with the guys.

Umm . . . pizza? With the guys? Pizza with the guys you work with all day? Pizza with the people you constantly see instead of having dinner with the woman you are about to marry and until today has lived 1,296 miles away? (Flashback: Once when I was in second grade I was swinging on the playground at recess and fell out of my swing. The swing went back up into the air and came down crashing against the back of my skull. This felt a lot like that.) I was all for pizza and all for the guys, but why did he not want to see me? I had no job. No friends. Nothing to do all day but wait for him to get off work and come over. The only reason I had made the move was so we could spend time together. To be with each other every day. To have dinner together on a Tuesday night. He should be dying to spend time with me. He should cancel everything unnecessary because the love of his life is finally in town. Instead he's aloof and disinterested. Aggravated that I asked. There seems to be an underlying annoyance that I would presume to alter his schedule in any way at all. Like somehow I should understand that my role is to be available when he wants me and to be silent at all other times. It shocks me that he could be so non-perfect at this moment. So selfish. So opposite of who I believed him to be.

I don't say a word the entire time we are at the grocery, silently putting things in the shopping cart and moving up and down the aisles in a daze. He halfheartedly asks once or twice what's wrong, but I pretend he isn't there. I can't focus. Don't want to think about this new person I am stuck with. Can't think about being alone in Boston with nowhere to go and nothing to do. No one to talk to. To me, it isn't just a stupid comment he made, it is his true self coming out. How he really feels. Who he is. I want to demand a refund. Shout that my purchase has a defect I hadn't noticed until now. But all purchases seem final, and I feel trapped.

> I feel confused. Terrified. Like I am stuck here with no way out and I might have to live my life like this.

Things steadily get worse over the next few days. I could go into detail, but who wants to relive every second of that again? I don't. The summary is that he continues to ignore me and act burdened by my presence. Continues to act like a completely different person. Continues to hurt me with slights and silences, generally overlooking me. I sit alone in the apartment all day wondering how I got here and how this happened. Wondering what I did to drive him away. Trying to come up with something, anything, to make sense of it all. Trying to remember how and when it started. But there is nothing. Somewhere along the way, he flipped a switch and that was that. I try to make the best of it. I put things away and clean the apartment. I never make us dinner because he won't eat. We celebrate Christmas with his family, and his friends take me to church, since he is working. Every moment

I feel confused. Terrified. Like I am stuck here with no way out and I might have to live my life like this. Smothered. Solemn. Next to a person who won't touch me or talk to me or really look at me. What have I done wrong?

Ross's friends plan a party for New Year's Eve, and I decide to bring some snacks. It is my one focus—my one activity to think about. Ross comes over after work and goes upstairs to take a nap, so I sit on the couch and wait for the clock to tell me it's time to start preparing for the party. Eventually he comes downstairs and sits next to me on the couch. More specifically, he sits at one end and I sit at the other and there's a long period of silence. Silence where there used to be so much to say. I ask him if he had a good nap, and he says he couldn't sleep. I ask him what's wrong, and he's silent. He doesn't move, doesn't look at me, doesn't seem to breathe. I ask him again, and he says he thinks he's depressed. I ask him why he might be depressed, and he says, "I think it's because you're here."

The oven timer dings. Time's up.

I ask him if he wants to postpone the wedding, confident that he'll say No. Knowing that he'll rush over to me and hold me and apologize for ever making me feel like he wouldn't want to marry me. Believing that with each moment that passes between us he will come to realize how much he needs me and loves me. Knowing that the mere thought of losing me will send him into a tailspin. Instead he just says Yes. Yes to postponing. He doesn't pause or think about it or cry. He just says Yes, as if it had been decided some time ago. He says he wants me to stay in Boston and continue to "date" him, but all I can hear is the Grim Reaper of Relationships pounding on the door. Suddenly time stops, and I feel as if I've drifted to the top of the room and am now observing everything from above. Like a dream. The words between us, which are few, sound muffled as if we are underwater. And I am sinking to the bottom.

I take off my engagement ring, which feels like removing a vital organ with no hope of a replacement. Like unplugging life support. He bursts into tears, and I'm not sure why. He's been silent as a stone until this moment. Maybe it's because taking off the ring symbolizes a severing. The severing of us. It's more than a ring—it's a life together. A promise to commit. They shouldn't call it an engagement ring because that sounds too romantic and carefree. They should call it a commitment ring. Binding. I wonder, if people sent to mental institutions were being "engaged" instead of "committed," would they happily oblige? Would it seem more pleasant? Would they call their friends and relatives and register for hospital gowns and craft supplies? I thought it would be different. I thought being in love and being engaged and being on the verge of the wedding would be different. But it wasn't. It was just like every other day, only I had new jewelry and a fancy party to plan. I thought being in love would solve some of the mystery in life. I thought it would make me feel pretty. But now I just feel hollow.

That night when he leaves he hugs me. It feels like hugging a stranger or an acquaintance that sorta creeps you out. Like dancing with the weird guy at the wedding because it's the wedding-party dance and he's your wedding-party counterpart. His arms are wrapped tightly around you and you can't escape without making a scene so you do your best to throw your head back, hoping to appear as if you're laughing but really you're trying to flee gracefully. I want to hug him and feel good. To feel like I once did. To feel safe and loved and together. Instead it feels wooden. Artificial. And I know that it's over.

His parents call and take me to lunch the next day. Casually, as if it's only Wednesday and not the first day of being broken up. No one mentions the obvious until I shout it out at the restaurant right as the waiter comes to wish us a Happy New Year. Happy New Year indeed. His parents, whom I love, beg me to stay in Boston. Beg me to wait it out. Beg me to do anything but leave. I tell them that Ross doesn't want me to be there anymore. That he believes me to be the source of his depression. That he won't talk to me and won't look at me and won't try. They cry and I cry and nothing is resolved. Everything is broken.

Everything is broken. I feel as if my subconscious is trying to figure out what happened. Looking for the warning signs I missed along the way.

The next day I drive four hours south to stay with my friend Laura. I couldn't face the emptiness in Boston. I've always been extremely independent and enjoyed being by myself. But this is different. This is . . . something worse than loneliness. Something much worse. While I'm driving I see our entire relationship flash before my eyes. Hearing his voice for the first time that summer afternoon while I was sitting on the patio of my favorite restaurant. Seeing him at the airport when I went to pick him up. He wore a black ribbed Gap shirt, Levi's, and an anxious look that I now recognize as fear. I remember his face when he asked me to marry him. I remember his face when he said never mind. I remember his laugh and his heart and his way with words. All of these images flash in my mind without warning or reasoning. I feel as if my subconscious is trying to figure out what happened. Looking for the warning signs I missed along the way.

But there is no answer to the riddle. No reason for his dismissal of me. He just decided he didn't want to marry me. And that was that. The beginning of the end of us. Or maybe just the end. It was definitely the end of my lifelong way of thinking. The end of believing that true love can begin in an instant. That romance comes complete with background music and a happy ending. It was definitely the beginning of discovering what I was made of. Discovering who it is that God created me to be.

Advice You Don't Want to Hear
After a Major Breakup

+ This too shall pass.

+ What doesn't break you makes you stronger. Just think about how strong you're going to be!

+ I knew all along that you two wouldn't work out.

+ Maybe you didn't pray enough.

+ I've got this cousin you would be perfect for. Should I give him your number?

+ There's lots of other fish in the sea.

+ Maybe you don't have enough faith.

+ You broke up? Well, what did you do? You must have done something to scare him off.

+ Don't start eating just because you're sad—you'll get fat.

+ Why are you so grouchy all the time?

+ He obviously wasn't the right one for you. You must have made the wrong choice.

+ Relationships are overrated anyway. You're much better off alone. (The word *alone* seems to reverberate . . . alone alone alone alone alone alone . . .)

✦ Did you nag him too much?

✦ You should really give him another chance. You're not getting any younger.

✦ Maybe you should get a makeover or lose a couple of pounds.

✦ Well you know, Jesus was single. Paul was too! I don't see what you're so upset about. Singleness is a calling.

✦ You aren't going to get a bunch of cats now, are you?

✦ Were you putting too much pressure on him?

✦ Just because you have a broken heart, don't let yourself go.

✦ I heard you broke up. That's too bad. Did you hear that Shelley just got engaged?

✦ Just think, things can't get any worse.

CHAPTER **THREE**

Rocky Mountain High

My friend Karina faced a mountain today. A hill I'm not sure I could climb. An old love showed up at church. An old love that she hadn't seen in two years because their relationship had ended badly. She knew he might be coming, knew he might be bringing a girl, and didn't hide out. She went to church and acted normal. I'm sure I would have slept in. Stayed in my hideout. Avoided him at all costs. But Karina faced the music. And when the old love walked in, she marched right up to him and said hello. She shook hands with his new girl and smiled. I think Karina might be the bravest woman I've ever met. Because she didn't let the past rule her life today. Today she faced it, said hello to it, and moved on. I, on the other hand, prefer to run.

I've tried my best to live my adult life void of Sunday school clichés. (You know, phrases like *Smile God Loves You* or *Christians Aren't Perfect, Just Forgiven* or *Turn or Burn.*) Not that all Sunday school clichés are necessarily bad, I just tend to avoid the obvious. And one of these aforementioned bumper-sticker sentimentalities is the "mountaintop experience." Yawn. I don't want to have a "retreat high" kind of faith. The very reason it's called a mountaintop experience is because the only direction left to go is down. You can't have a mountaintop experience without the follow-up downhill dive. I don't want to be hot and cold with long periods of warm. I don't want my life to be based on a series of moments that were spectacular and view the rest as ho-hum. I don't want to feel the need to attend a seminar or camp or concert to find God. I'd rather find Him in the everyday. Therefore, I avoid the mountaintop highs as best I can. I prefer every moment to be real and true. Simply said, I prefer life, not moments.

And life is exactly what I've had this past year. A broken heart and a canceled wedding and a move back to Nashville. The list seems endless. There's too much to take in and hurt from and think about and process through and get over and on with. On the weekend that I should have been getting married, everything seemed too overwhelming. Anticipating this, AJ and I had discussed going on a trip to ease the passing of the inevitable weekend. It just so happened that one of our bands (we both work for a record company) was playing a show that weekend in Seattle, so we decided to go.

I went to Seattle to try to think about other things. To live my current life and do my job and hang out with my friends and move on. To try to forget that he forgot me. To try to erase the pain of my current low. The valley that I must trudge through. So AJ and I filled our schedule to the brim with "fun" activities that would surely soften the blow of moments missed. I guess I assumed if I was doing something fun, I would forget about the exact moment I should have been at my rehearsal dinner, the exact moment the church doors should have opened and I would walk down the aisle to forever, the exact moment I should have finally been alone with my new husband. These are the things I most wanted to overlook. To run from. And run I did.

Our flight out of Nashville was delayed and we had a layover in Minneapolis. Actually, it wasn't a layover. It was more like a moment or two to get from plane A to plane B with no time to spare. The longer our Nashville flight was delayed, the more worried AJ and I became. Missing a flight was not part of the perfect weekend plan. Our flight finally arrived, took off, and landed in Minneapolis with twenty minutes to spare. Sounds like plenty unless you've been to the Minneapolis airport (a.k.a. a small city in Minnesota). The connecting flight was several terminals away and we had to run for it. And by run, I mean *run*. Sprint. Like being chased by the bad guy or a large rabid dog. My energy level was low due to the emotional wreckage in my heart, so I lasted about a minute. However, there wasn't time to rest. So we ran. And ran. And ran. We made it to the gate just as the final boarding call was being announced. And I nearly fainted. Flight attendants were concerned for my health. I was concerned about breathing normally. I sat down and drank some water, buckled my seat belt and began the countdown. Two more days to get through.

Friday, the rehearsal dinner day, AJ and I planned to attend a radio interview with one of our bands, drive to Crystal Mountain to go skiing, go to a rock-'n'-roll show, attend a book signing at a local store—and avoid all talk of weddings. The day was to begin at 6:30 AM and end around 2:00 AM. There was definitely not going to be enough time to dwell on what could have been or what should have been. What I was missing. Everything went as planned. I arrived at the radio station and the band did well in the interview. I met new people and shook their hands and smiled. I told jokes and laughed. I drove to the mountain with AJ, singing and dancing along the way. We arrived at the mountain and I put on my borrowed ski jacket, rented smelly ski boots and skis. This would be my first experience skiing, which made the activity a perfect distraction. I'd be too busy thinking about how to stop the skis to dwell on how I should have been getting married.

My friends were all skiers of some accomplished level, but all were patient and helped me on the bunny slope. I've always heard that skiing is hard but extremely fun. After about an hour, I wondered when the fun would kick in. I attempted to make the skis work as they should, only to fall down repeatedly. And I couldn't get up. At all. All very good distractions. But I still had a pit in my stomach. I still had a hollow feeling. I still, unintentionally, checked my watch to know what time it should have been. And I began to feel defeated. What was I doing in Seattle on a mountain wearing smelly ski boots, lying in the snow unable to get up? I shouldn't be here! I should be getting married!

It was decided that we would all meet back at the lodge for lunch around noon. I wasn't hungry, but was grateful for the break. After lunch a group of us decided to abandon the dreaded skis and attempt to snowboard. Right. Either way, I would be locking my feet onto something unnatural and placing myself perilously on a slope made of ice and snow. (I also suspect the ski rental dudes greased my board especially slick when they learned I was a first-timer.) I had tired of trying to ski, and snowboarding looked much easier, so I was in. My friend, Will, an experienced snowboarder, accepted the challenge to teach AJ and me the basics. On each of us, he locked one foot onto the snowboard and put us on the ski lift to *the top of the mountain*. Wait! Shouldn't we start on the bunny slope with the rest of the beginners? Shouldn't there be some sort of lesson or trial period or points to remember? Will sat us on the ski lift as we shouted these very questions. The higher we went, the drier my mouth got. The steeper the mountain became, the more my insides quivered.

Challenge #1: Get off the ski lift. This was a skill we had not learned, or even attempted. I watched nervously as friends in front of me attempted to slide off gracefully but instead fell with a thud, one after the other. Not wanting to go against the flow, I fell off the chair lift with a hard thud. (Is this where the fun begins?) I tumbled to the starting line as Will locked my other foot onto the snowboard. He gave AJ and me a few cryptic instructions that everyone else seemed to understand and shooshed down the mountain.

> I hadn't allowed myself to be alone all day. Hadn't given myself the opportunity to spend time with the obvious. Now here I was, really alone.

About an hour later, I was still at the top of the mountain. Sure, I had made it part of the way down. Or rather, *rolled* part of the way down. But, essentially, I was still at the top. I imagined that AJ was much farther down and having a great time. Maybe she understood the concepts a bit better than I did. I was left all alone at the top of a cold mountain with a board locked to my feet, sitting in the snow, feeling lost. I hadn't allowed myself to be alone all day. Hadn't given myself the opportunity to spend time with the obvious. Now here I was, *really* alone.

When you are at the top of a mountain, there's no noise except for the occasional swoosh of a snowboarder racing past you so fast your hair blows. It's even quieter than a library. At least at the library there are loud kids screaming for Mommy and old guys who breathe too loud and books that drop on the hardwood floor. Up on the mountain, it was truly silent. I sat there wondering what I was going to do to get off that ridiculous mountain. Every ounce of what little energy I had that day had been used trying to mask my disappointment. My longing to be somewhere else. I had run out of steam, patience, and will. I was lying there, in the snow, with a snowboard clamped to my feet and my eyes shut tight in an attempt to hold back tears desperately trying to surface.

I lay there for a long time. My mind raced with all that had happened in the past year. The past three months. The past hour. I thought about how much I had loved Ross and how much he had hurt me. I thought about how unfair it all seemed and wondered how I was going to get through it. Sure, I was doing okay. Going to work every day and fulfilling obligations and spending time with friends. But the empty echo inside me rang louder. I was not, contrary to what I told everyone, fine.

> And although I wasn't trying to listen, although I was shutting Him out, I heard God speaking into my life. Telling me that my life isn't always what I think it should be.

After a long while, I opened my eyes and looked around, truly looked around. The sky was a pure blue and the sun was shining. All the colors seemed vivid and alive. I was sitting on a mountaintop. The scenery was beautiful, unlike anything I've seen before. And although I wasn't trying to listen, although I was shutting Him out, I heard God speaking into my life. Telling me that my life isn't always what I think it should be. That things aren't always as they seem. That the marriage I was missing wasn't the marriage intended for me. That being in Seattle stuck on a mountaintop was far better than marrying the wrong person.

It had been easy for me to mourn what could have been and overlook what actually was. But I realized up there that in the midst of my heartbreak, I was actually being saved from far worse. I never would have experienced this mountain had it not been for the valley. The only reason I was still enough and quiet enough to hear Him was because of the acute pain I was running from. Intently set on running from the hurt, I ran straight into this view. This quiet. An encounter with my God. It took a literal mountaintop experience to fully believe that I was in the right place. I don't know why it took me running to Seattle to find that out, but I finally got it.

It's funny how God tends to work in my life. Funny that He would take a girl who scoffs at religious highs to the top of a mountain so that I could experience Him. Hear Him. So that I could understand that life isn't unfair, just unexpected. That He really does know exactly where I am, and He won't let me fall.

CHAPTER **FOUR**

Nine Times a Bridesmaid

A friend just came by my office to hug me and to say good job. Normally, this would make me exuberant and want to hug myself in congratulatory rapture. I might even buy myself some job-well-done ice cream, pop open a Diet Coke, and proclaim this a day of cheer. Might even post a sign on my door letting everyone know what a great job I did. I'm in sales, so I'm not exactly humble in my accomplishments. Part of what I do is shout about the good stuff. Holler that we're #1! I should wear an "F" for Flicker Records on my sweater and carry pompoms. I should have a hip-clip for my bullhorn and paint the company logo on my cheek. (I work there, by the way.)

But alas, this wasn't one of those occasions. When my friend left my office, I wanted to slam the door and hide. I wanted to put my phone on Do Not Disturb and lay under my desk. Climb out the window. Shimmy down the drainpipe. Run away. Because I can handle all this breakup stuff as long as no one addresses it. As long as it's a secret. The past is easier to ignore if no one knows. And lately, sometimes, people forget since everything is back to the way it was. Some people even forget that I left and came back again. Everything is back in its place and there's a smile on my face. Everything is the way it should have been, the way that makes everyone around me feel safe and relieved. Me too. I'm glad it's sometimes hard to remember that I left. But then today a friend came in my office to hug me and to say good job.

The hug was prompted by last night, no doubt. Last night I threw an engagement party for my friends Steve and AJ. (Turns out the long-distance thing works for some people after all.) The hugger came in and said he was "impressed" by my attitude lately and was "proud" of me for being so "brave." I suppose my bravery is due to the fact that I was engaged myself, a few moments ago. Or a few months ago. Depends on your perspective. I guess he was in awe of me for being happy for someone else getting what was taken from me. Yes—throwing an engagement party soon after my own engagement went belly up is not my idea of rowdy fun. Wearing a bridesmaid's dress for the ninth time in my life sounds like the premise of a trashy summer novel. But, yes, the happiness of others is sometimes more important than my own. Yes, I am able to see past my own wound to revel in the happiness of those whom I love. At least occasionally. I will admit—it's very hard. I'm just trying to figure it out on my own; trying to see what works and what doesn't. Sometimes I'm happy, truly happy. Sometimes I'm thrilled. And sometimes I feel that I might break into a million pieces right in front of their eyes. Might crumble. Might fall down dead.

The worst thing you can do right after your wedding has

been called off is participate in someone else's wedding. (By worst I mean the absolute worst most awful to the one-hundredth degree very very bad no good thing you can do.) (It's bad.) So of course, that is exactly what I'm doing. It's not bad because Steve and AJ are happy and good things are happening for them and not for me. It's wedding envy. Goofy love envy. Honeymoon envy.

A few months after Ross and I broke up, Steve e-mailed me that he was going to propose to AJ soon and needed a woman's advice. I was just that woman. Still reeling from my breakup and still mourning the loss of my own wedding, I thought, *Hey, why not?* Steve and I went over various ideas for the proposal—me shooting down most of his ideas and dramatically playing up mine in an effort to convince him that there was no other option.

My own proposal from Ross . . . well . . . stunk. It was all wrong. Nothing I would have ever wanted or dreamed of or wished for. I decided immediately, even while he was asking, that I wouldn't care. That there are more important things in life than the quality of the proposal. And while I still think it's true, that there are more important things, I wonder if it should have been a sign. A red light. Something to notice. To me, a proposal should be fireworks and lightning and a march-ing band that suddenly comes down the street. Instead, Ross's proposal was a question like, *Will you stop at the store and pick up some milk, please?* Should I have hesitated? Should I have questioned? Was it really a sign of things to come?

Since there had been no marching band for me, I had some sort of insane inner force driving me to make sure

Steve's proposal to AJ was the most magnificent, fabulous moment in the history of all proposals ever. And I honestly did consider what AJ would like and dislike. It wasn't entirely driven by insanity. Just kinda sorta.

So Steve and I settled on a plan. I would propose a fake cookout at our friend Bob's house and Steve would be out of town on a fake work trip. Brilliant, I know. I would suggest to AJ that we go over to Steve's house to watch a movie after the cookout since Steve would be out of town and he has a big TV. (Steve had unselfishly moved to Nashville from Boston months earlier.) However, Steve would be waiting at the apartment with candles, flowers, and the ring. AJ would be none the wiser.

The day of the proposal I was a wreck. I knew she would see it in my face and discover the secret. Steve, being the genius that he is, checked the weather channel and called AJ from "Atlanta" and said that it was a nice day, but cloudy. At lunch I went to Costco and bought every red and white rose they had. I had borrowed about fifty candles from my roommate and took them and the roses over to Steve's, constantly checking the rearview mirror. I felt like a spy. A double agent. I should have thought to give myself a code name like Agent Engagement or Thorny Rose. I got to Steve's and we set up the candles and pulled the petals off the roses to spread on the floor. Things were going perfectly. That night AJ and I went to the fraudulent cookout. We left early and went over to Steve's . . . and well, the rest was as it should be. Steve said, *Will you?* and AJ said, *Yes!* And I was truly, truly happy for them. Then I cried all the way home.

There's a big church on the corner of an intersection I often drive through. On Saturdays there's always a wedding at this big church on the corner. Sometimes two. I know this because the side of the sanctuary that faces the busy road has a long row of about five or six enormous picture windows. I can see inside. And when I drive past my view is straight to the altar. I wonder if the church builders planned it this way. I wonder if the happy couples know that all of West Nashville can see their private moment . . . at least for a second or two. I've seen all different stages of weddings at this church on the corner. I've seen florists putting bows on the aisles and setting up the brass candelabras. I've seen guests milling around the parking lot after the ceremony. I've seen the bride posing on the front steps with her bridesmaids. Once, while driving past at twilight, the entire sanctuary was lit with candles and the father of the bride was giving away his daughter to the groom. I witnessed this right after moving back to Nashville from Boston and almost had to pull my car over, it was so overwhelming. My wedding was going to be candlelit. My father was going to give me away.

I wonder what it is about seeing weddings that can make a single girl's stomach turn. Envy? Bitterness? Jealousy? Loneliness? Maybe all of the above. We rarely feel total happiness for the bride. If we do, it's delusional at best. Today I was planning to meet my roommate Jen at the gym. She called and said she was running a bit late, so I decided to watch TV for the extra few minutes. A movie was on and I started watching right as the big wedding scene began. I've seen this movie many times before—so why in the world did I start crying? I was glad I was alone because I felt like a psycho. Because it wasn't phone commercial sniffling; I was wailing. I didn't even know why. I wanted to scratch the bride's eyes out and knock over the candelabras. I wanted to pull the blooms off all her pretty flowers and stomp on them with big muddy boots. I wanted to be the one getting married. I wanted to wear the enviable dress and have the gorgeous hair. I wanted to change the channel. But I didn't. I just kept watching.

Several months before the wedding, I began having disturbing dreams about weddings. I tend to have disturbing dreams anyway, but the wedding dreams were new. And in these disturbing dreams I was always the bride—or at least always wearing a wedding dress. Once I was sent into a room with David Schwimmer, the actor. My job was to seduce him and get some information that he had. The weird dream twist was that I was wearing a wedding dress. I think it's quite a known fact that no seducing could be done while wearing a wedding dress. Another dream featured me, yet again, wearing a wedding dress and participating in espionage. I wore a gold and green velvet wedding gown that zipped from toe to neck. And a long long veil with colored jewels. I had very short, very frizzy, very red hair. I was an actor and was apparently supposed to marry another actor. It's someone well known but I can't remember his name or any movies he's been in. He had salt-and-pepper hair, was ruggedly handsome, and had nice lips. I remember he was quite concerned about me looking the part in order to fool the enemy. I was concerned about my frizzy hair not working with the veil. Just then the bad guys walked in and the game was up. We were discovered. It wasn't violent or anything like that. We were just sad and took off our costumes.

I don't quite understand wedding envy, but I've always had it. My roommate Karina applied for a job once and was asked to draw her wildest dream. They didn't provide any other explanation than that and gave her a blank sheet of paper and everything. So she drew herself getting married. (And didn't get the job.) Maybe I'm taking this too far, but I think society brainwashes women to crave weddings. And this definition of society isn't just the media, it's our mothers and our grand-mothers and our aunts and our friends and sometimes our childhood pediatricians. What little girl hasn't played "wed-ding" and thought about what hers will be like and giggled when her grandma says, *Someday you'll get married too!*

> I think society brainwashes women to crave weddings. If weddings weren't tradition, would we pine away wanting to get married?

I laughed when Monica on the TV show *Friends* got engaged to Chandler and pulled out her wedding book that she had been making since she was a kid. I laughed because years before she met Chandler she had picked out her col-ors and her flowers and her dress. I laughed, but I have a book too. Every girl I know has thought about what her wedding dress will look like and who her bridesmaids will be since . . . well, since forever. I think it starts when we learn to talk. For me, college was the worst because that's when my friends started getting married. I could get close. I could go with them to the bridal shop and try things on. I could look at flowers with them and talk about reception food, even though I wasn't the one having the wedding. And I wanted it—bad. It's maddening. I've known friends who went on a first date with a guy and the next day bought bride magazines "just to dream" about their wedding to him. And that's the problem. It's a dream. A fantasy. One that may or may not come true. One that can get so blown out of proportion that it's unobtainable.

It makes me wonder. If weddings weren't tradition, would we pine away wanting to get married? What if to get married, a girl and her intended were only required to meet with their pastor and talk over a few things and all pray together and that was it? That's really the core of a wedding—the commitment. Everything else is icing on the wedding cake. And I *love* the icing. I want it all. I want the dress and the flowers and the candles and the vows and the reception. I've literally thought about that day since I began eating solid foods. But, the wedding is not the marriage. (Exercise: Repeat ten times aloud that "the wedding is not the marriage.") I think that fact can sometimes get forgotten in the hoopla. Marriage is commitment and forgiveness and arguments and money management and forever. Typically, weddings are glorified parties.

I'm trying to think back to how I felt when Ross and I

broke up. I'll admit, half of my anger was due to the canceled wedding, not the canceled marriage. I was on the verge of getting my dream wedding and he backed out! The jerk! But what about the marriage? The lifetime commitment? Did I think about that? I did. Sometimes. Okay, a lot. But I also thought about my dress that I wouldn't get to wear and the flowers I wouldn't get to carry and my friends I had wanted to stand beside me. I get nervous that the breakup would have been easier if a wedding hadn't been involved. If all that was canceled was a marriage, I think I might have been relieved instead of angry. I think. Who knows. Is that crazy? Do other people feel this way?

I've been thinking about couples I know who have been married for quite some time. They rarely, if ever, talk about the wedding. Now it's about life and getting on with it—together. It's about who feeds the kids and who takes out the trash and how much money is left at the end of the month and let's go to Home Depot and whose family will we visit for Christmas. It's about life being lived together. And that should be the focus. That should be the goal. I don't want to commit myself to someone because he'll look good in a tux in wedding photos. I want to commit myself to someone who will walk through life with me. Someone who will love me unconditionally. Or will at least try.

It's scary what some girls will do in pursuit of the perfect wedding. If Christian universities offered a major in Wifeology or an elective class called "The Perfect Wedding," I wonder how many girls would enthusiastically enroll. Loads, surely. It's embarrassing how many girls I knew who entered college with absolutely no intention of ever having a career or even a job. They were simply on a manhunt. They would major in things like Psychology and Early Childhood Development. I guess this made them more prepared to be a wife and mother? And being a wife and mother is a wonderful thing—I hope to be both someday. But life is not about who gets married first and fanciest. It's not about what man you catch. Sadly, some of these Man Hunters captured their prey. I say sadly because some of these marriages are now in ruin. Which isn't to say that they all are; some are happy and content and wonderful. My point is that some girls were shocked to learn that marriage doesn't equal a happy life. And I am shocked to find that I am happier than some of these girls who actually landed a man. Me—the spinster. Unlucky in love. But I'm happier!

I've had several friends over the years who have said that they didn't really want to be married, they just wanted to have a wedding. Wanted to be the bride for once. Wanted to feel like a princess. Sometimes I would nod yes and say, *Uh-huh, me too.* I wonder if planning a phony wedding would cure this insatiable desire within. What if? What if I spent the big bucks and threw myself a fabulous wedding? What if I got out my wedding book and fulfilled every wish? What if I invited all my family and friends and went through with the whole fabulous thing? And what if at the altar I stood next to a rented stand-in? An actor. A good-looking mannequin even. I could sit next to the mannequin at the equally fabulous reception and could stand next to him in photos. Sounds delightful. Sounds perfect. Right?

After AJ's engagement (the very perfectly planned, orchestrated, and successful engagement, I might add), she asked me to be her maid of honor. I was honored and terrified all at once. I know what it means to be in a wedding—I've been a bridesmaid eight times before—and I wasn't sure that this particular stage of my life was the most appropriate time to dive right in to the Wonderful World of Weddings. I knew that participating in someone else's wedding could be painful and hard and traumatic. I knew that there was a possibility that Ross could be involved in the wedding as well. I knew that saying yes would most likely be an incredibly bad idea. So I said yes.

AJ's Malibu beach wedding was beautiful and perfect. The sun was shining and the wind was blowing. The ocean was beautiful and the bride was even more beautiful. Her friends and family were there and all was well with the world. Right before the ceremony I was running around pinning boutonnieres on the groom and the groomsmen and fathers and pastors. I was putting cameras on the tables and giving the all-clear sign for the wedding party to start walking down the aisle. I hadn't had time to think about what was happening to me. When it was my turn, I slowly walked down the aisle, mentally checking everyone's flowers and position. The sun was shining at the exact place in the sky that AJ wanted. Check. The videographer was hidden to the side. Check. The groom was next to the pastor. Check. I took my place at the front and turned to see AJ walk down the aisle with her father. She was truly breathtaking. And I felt fine. I did. AJ walked down the aisle and

I began to think that all my worrying had been in vain. It was fine. I was fine. Until the part with the vows.

> Every girl wants a guy to love her. Every girl wants him to sweep her off her feet and ask her to marry him.

I finally get why everyone wants a wedding. I get the allure. It's the moment. Standing in front of everyone you love and telling the one person you love the most exactly why you love them. It's publicly proclaiming before God and the rest that you vow yourself to this person. You promise to love and cherish and honor and deal. It's about the promise you make to each other. It's not about cake or dresses or favors. It's about commitment.

I guess Ross wasn't ready to make that commitment to me. I was. I had already written my vows. I believed, at the time, that I was ready to say them and mean them. But now—who knows? It's hard to say. So much time has passed and too many things are left unsaid. But being in this wedding showed me one thing. It really isn't the canceled wedding that broke my heart. It's the canceled commitment. His unwillingness to stick it out. His apathy toward us. He didn't just quit the wedding, he quit me. That's the part that hurts the most. I don't want a fake wedding with a handsome mannequin. I want someone to love me so much that it bursts right out of him. I want someone who is willing to go through the wedding lunacy because he wants everyone to know that he is committed to loving me for life.

And that's why being in AJ and Steve's wedding was hard. Because they get it. They love each other and have chosen to make the commitment.

Every girl wants a guy to love her. Every girl wants him to sweep her off her feet and ask her to marry him. I had him. Then I lost him. All those years of wishing and dreaming and planning, I never considered what to do if I lost it all at the last minute. What I should do if he changed his mind. I didn't have a Plan B. So what was I supposed to do next?

CHAPTER **FIVE**

Lost and Found

I love riding in cars with boys, especially at night on the interstate. I don't know why. It's not something I can describe; it just makes me feel happy. Safe. Liked. Maybe I love how the dashboard lights illuminate his face or how his hand looks on the gear shift. Maybe I like the comfortable silence. I know that riding in a car with a boy doesn't make me liked or safe. Still, I like it. I miss it. When I think back to times when I've ridden with boys in cars late at night, the memories always seem peaceful. But Wednesday night I was driving alone at night on the interstate. I turned up the radio and rolled down the window to drown out the sound of being alone. Single Silence. Breakup Silence. It might actually be the loudest sound I've ever heard. And that's when it happened.

I was unsuccessfully fighting traffic in Nashville to get to my parents' house for Thanksgiving. I love Thanksgiving— it's one of my favorite holidays. I love the weather and the food and the . . . well mostly the weather and the food. And the merriment. It's cold outside, but not too cold. And it's only one day—not an entire month like Christmas. (Enough already!) Everyone seems to be in the holiday mood. Your boss lets you knock off early. Your mom makes your favorite dishes and desserts. No one cares if you take a four-hour nap—it's even encouraged. Thanksgiving rules. And Wednesday night, driving through Nashville traffic mayhem, I was excited. Excited to see my brother and my family and have a good meal and just hang out. But I ended up stuck in traffic for more than two hours.

Last year I went to Boston to spend Thanksgiving with Ross's family. Flying the day before Thanksgiving can be quite an adventure, especially when you're flying alone. And especially when you tend to be thrifty when purchasing plane tickets and therefore have to change planes three times before reaching your final destination. I was in four airports that day and delayed three times. I thought Thanksgiving might even be over by the time I got there. But I did finally arrive and things went according to plan. The weekend was wonderful, magical even. He wanted to be with me and couldn't get enough of me and loved every moment with me. Thanksgiving was kisses and loving looks and time and laughter. Thanksgiving was great.

I remember seeing him that night at the airport after traveling the entire day. I ran straight into his arms and stayed there for awhile. He had been waiting for me for quite some time and the reunion was grand, just short of him twirling me in slow motion. (Come to think of it, why didn't he twirl me?) He knew I would be hungry and had brought me Dunkin' Donuts, which I took as the sweetest gesture any man had ever bestowed on any woman. I was either starry-eyed, jet-lagged, or deliriously in love. Maybe all three.

But this year I would be with my family. And I was feeling good about that. Satisfied. I had the holiday spirit. On the drive up I had been thinking about everything going on in my life—and how much had changed. Last Thanksgiving I was engaged and ecstatic and sure of our love and our life together. Ross and me—so right and so natural. But this year was different and I was doing all right. Some might even say that I have an enviable life! A great job and great family and great friends. Then I took the exit for my parents' house and "our song" came on the radio. Our song that I hadn't heard since we broke up. And that's when it happened.

Enter The Void.

The Void is that deep chasm of loneliness that surprises you at precisely the worst imaginable moment. Like when I arrived at my parents' house for Thanksgiving and everyone was inside waiting for me but I couldn't go in because I had just heard "our song" on the radio and then I started crying and didn't want to explain to everyone why I was crying because all they would hear is that I miss him and think I'm pathetic and sad. The Void is like that. Squelcher of Holiday Cheer.

One advantage I had in breaking up with Ross is that he lives in Boston and I live in Nashville. I don't run into him while on a date or see him at church. He isn't in my circle of friends. I don't know his new girlfriend (does he have one?) and I don't know if he's happy or sad or if he cares about what happened. I don't know if he still lives in the same place and I don't know how his parents are doing and I don't run into his sister at the gym. All of these things, I realize, are extreme privileges and I do not take them for granted. I've had friends who worked for their Ex or lived next door to their Ex—or, worst of all, whose pastor was her Ex. Ugh. I have no comprehension of what it would be like to have to casually run into Ross. To have to make polite conversation and act nonchalant and unaffected. I think I would give myself away. I would probably be mean or act like I didn't see him or pretend to flirt with someone else.

The meanest part of The Void is that it has no agenda or schedule. I can't plan for it. It's always a shock . . . it steals my breath away. Makes me gasp. It can be a commercial on TV or a song or a smell. A photograph hidden in a drawer. All I want is some lousy Scotch tape and instead I'm flooded with a memory so haunting I think he's in the room with me. Sometimes I wish he were there. Sometimes I'm glad he's not.

The Void also shows up when something desirable happens to someone else. I don't know why, but lately there's been a rash of flower deliveries in my office. My office window faces the parking lot and I can see them pull up. I see the flower delivery guy get out and open the back of the van and retrieve some gorgeous arrangement intended for someone in my building. Each time I think it could be something from Ross. Something saying he's sorry. Saying he wants me back. Or maybe flowers from a secret admirer. Someone who has loved me from afar, but I was engaged to another. Each time I hope it's for me. Each time it isn't.

Lost and Found

What does it even mean—The Void? I think it's interesting that personal checks are void after ninety days. Like the big bad bank is challenging me to get that check deposited before it's too late. Before time runs out. My paychecks are void immediately. I have direct deposit (that I love), which means my biweekly salary goes directly to the bank. However, I do get a faux check that shows the amount that was deposited on my behalf and says that the faux check is void. It's not a check. It's not negotiable and not worth anything. It's void.

When a retail cashier makes a mistake, she has to call a manager over to void the sale. To delete it. To expunge it from the system. To start over. To me, this—The Void—is the worst part of breaking up. A void is a lack of contents that should be present. It's emptiness.

I was putting something in the trunk of my car the other day and found some torn wrapping paper with a Christmas tag attached that said: "To JoAnna, Love, Ross." (Okay, so I don't clean out my trunk very often.) Seeing the words "love" and "Ross" next to each other made my stomach churn. Seeing my name in his serial-killer-perfect handwriting made my eyes water. I wonder what he finds? Is he still using the Crest spinbrush I gave him for Christmas? (Of all the gifts, the seven-dollar toothbrush was his favorite.) What did he do with our photos or all the cards I mailed him? I wonder what his family did with the Christmas gifts from me? Does he stumble upon some evidence of me when he least expects it? While cleaning out his deleted e-mails does he come across a forgotten one from me? Does it make him sad? Angry? Does he miss me? Does he feel The Void?

At a party the other night I was sitting on a crowded sectional sofa. My friend Michelle was sitting next to me and her new boyfriend came over and sat beside her. He put his arm around her waist, and due to the overcrowding, he was practically touching me too. For some reason, it made my heart sad and my cheeks burn. It made me recognize The Void. I have a friend who went through a massive breakup not long ago and has had to deal with The Void, too. In what I presume was an attempt to move on, she used to go to "their" restaurant and sit in "their" booth alone. And she'd cry. Was she inviting The Void to dinner? I have another friend who dated someone she was presumed to marry. Instead they broke up and he married someone else. My friend now hangs out with the wife and says it's fine—says they're even friends. I don't believe her.

The Void seems to be responsible for so many things. Feeling alone. Crying at night. Sometimes it even causes people to stay together for the wrong reasons. Some girls would rather be with someone who lies to them than face The Void alone. Fortunately, I'm not that bad off. Yet. I'm still in the fight, wrestling the battle of the empty echo. The hollow thump. Because breaking up is losing your best friend. Your last call of the day. Your Valentine. Your New Year's kiss at midnight. And sometimes, the person you expect to spend your life with. When I lost Ross, I lost more than a Friday night date. I lost it all, or at least it felt like I did. My entire future was wrapped up in him—and then he was gone. It made me not want to trust anyone else, including God. Everyone says to run to God in times of heartbreak—but that was sometimes the last place I wanted to go. At that time, even a relationship with God seemed scary. What if He abandons me too? What if He leaves?

My friend Josh Bales wrote a song that says more about The Void than I ever could. This song seems to have dipped into the deepest part of my heart to reach the feelings even I can't see. It's a song about not always being able to accept the love God has to give. About loss and being hurt and how it's difficult to trust again. Difficult to love again. I asked Josh if I could share his wise words, and he said okay:

"About a Boy"
by Josh Bales

You mention things I dare not wonder
Whisper words my heart can't say
How I'd love to hold You closer
I would if not for all these chains

I know that You know that there's something
I'm not telling You
I'm just a boy who lost his best friend
Nothing You can do

When will You force me to love You
When will my heart give in
I know I can't stay here forever but
I'm too scared to just jump in

I see a thousand caring faces
When I'm in bed at night
It's funny how our fears of darkness
Can turn into fears of light

Will You come down
And wrap Your arms around me
And when I cringe
Just let me know You won't let go

He's right. It's hard to trust—even hard to trust something proven. Hard to open up. Hard to leap. Hard to accept unconditional love from someone so holy and good. Hard to believe I'm lovable. If Ross couldn't even love me, how could anyone else? There have been times when I've been so afraid of something else bad happening, I even become afraid of something good happening. Intense heartbreak changes your outlook. Relationships shift and trust becomes the enemy. God becomes a confusing figure who feels unsafe. At least that's what happens to me. My fear of darkness turns into a fear of light.

My friend Rob told me his story about finding The One. He was about twenty-four years old and his friend Chad called him up one day and said he'd found The One. This unnerved Rob. Like until that moment he had been fine living life as is and didn't feel any need to look for The One. But now Chad had met The One and Rob was being left behind. Immediately Rob began his hot pursuit of finding The One. Just so happens that Rob was dating a girl at the time—who became The One for him. That forever love lasted only a short time and then dissolved. Chad's relationship with his love dissolved quickly too. What happened?

Maybe there comes a certain point for many of us when we think it's about time to get something going. It's about time to be in love and settle down. Maybe the first person that manages to stumble in our general direction becomes our greatest heart's desire. I wonder . . . is this what Ross did? Did he think it was about time he fell in love and I happened along? Did he want to get married before he reached a certain age and thought I would fit the bill well enough? Did he tell me he loved me just so he could tell someone? I don't know. I don't think I'll ever know.

Maybe he never meant all the things he said to me. Maybe they were just things he had always wanted to say. Maybe they were just things I wanted to say—and to hear in return. Maybe the lines between what's real and what we believe is expected of us are invisible. Maybe our current surroundings have left us wanting. It's almost as if I can tell someone that I love him, but unless he says he loves me too, I feel incomplete. We see our friends proclaim love to another and think we have to be next. Our turn has to be coming up. And The Void grows—and makes us feel lost. Displaced. Overlooked.

Ross's words meant something to me. And they left an emptiness in me when taken away. I didn't think it was possible for someone to tell me that he loved me forever and then change his mind. Never expected someone to ask me to marry him and then say no thanks. I also didn't anticipate the barren wasteland that my heart would become. The well of loneliness so deep there wasn't room for anyone but me.

For me, that's the worst part. Feeling lonely and lost. After breaking up with Ross and moving back to Nashville, I felt like I didn't belong. My friends were glad to see me, but we had already said good-bye. My roommates had already replaced me in the house. I walked into work my first day back and the new intern had taken over my office. People who ran into me at the movies would ask how married life was—I had to say I didn't know. I didn't belong in Nashville, and I didn't belong in Boston. And I didn't belong anywhere else. I was lost.

My roommate Karina and I recently moved into a house with our friends Tiffany and Jen. Before the move I was sorting things that were already packed—like Christmas decorations and old photographs. (These boxes stay packed from move to move and I only look through them when packing to move again.) I was going through these boxes and realized that something was missing. A few Christmases ago, my mom had given me some Christmas dishes that I loved. I hadn't used them in a few years because I had been moving and traveling and living in a house with a million girls and kept most things packed away in the basement. And then when I finally looked for them, they were gone. I have no idea how long they have been missing or when they got lost. I wasn't sad that the dishes were missing until I looked for them. I didn't realize they were gone until I searched.

Jesus always told great stories when He was on earth. It's one of my favorite things about Him. And one of His great stories is in Luke 15, the story of the lost sheep. Actually it's more of a "what if." Jesus is talking to some religious leaders whose only goal was to trip Him up and get Him to say something wrong. *The Message* tells the story like this:

> *By this time a lot of men and women of doubtful reputation were hanging around Jesus, listening intently. The Pharisees and religion scholars were not pleased, not at all pleased. They growled, "He takes in sinners and eats meals with them, treating them like old friends." Their grumbling triggered this story. "Suppose one of you had a hundred sheep and lost one." (vv. 1–4)*

Maybe Jesus looked around at this point to see what the religious suits were thinking. Made sure they were listening. Then He goes on to say,

> *Wouldn't you leave the ninety-nine in the wilderness and go after the lost one until you found it? When found, you can be sure you would put it across your shoulders, rejoicing, and . . . saying, "Celebrate with me! I've found my lost sheep!" Count on it— there's more joy in heaven over one sinner's rescued life than over ninety-nine good people in no need of rescue. (vv. 4–7)*

And that's what Jesus said. That if one is missing, the shepherd would surely go and look for the missing sheep. The lost sheep. The sheep who wasn't missing until the shepherd went to look for him. Maybe that's me. Maybe

I'm not really lost. Maybe I'm not really out here wandering all alone. Maybe He's looking for me.

My roommate heard a story in church today about a Native American tradition between father and son. When a boy reached the age of about eleven or twelve, his father would blindfold him and lead him out into the woods. The boy would then be left alone in the woods all night. Now, you might think staying all night in the woods alone wasn't a big deal for this young boy (as I did), but apparently it was. These boys had never been alone in their entire lives. At all. I guess it's true that teepees don't have separate rooms for kids. So as part of becoming a man, a boy would have to fend for himself all night in the woods. Alone.

The woods are scary at night. Especially when you are alone. There are strange noises and rustlings and you can't see. It's dark. In the night the young Indian hears the growls of bears and the prowling of panthers. He hears sounds he's never heard before. It's a sleepless, restless night full of rustlings and shadows and unknowns. Scary stuff. But he has to stick it out. He has to make it to morning.

Eventually morning comes and the boy discovers that he's made it all night. He's okay—and he has become a man to his tribe! He gets up and looks around only to see his father standing in the trees—his father who had led him out into the woods to be alone. His father who secretly stayed there, all night, watching over him. His father who had a bow and arrow ready to protect his son from any harm. Turns out the boy wasn't alone after all.

The Void can feel like that. Spending all night alone in the woods. Hearing strange whispers and creepy rustlings and seeing moving shadows. It's dark and unfamiliar—and lonely. But . . . maybe that's me. Maybe I'm not really lost. Maybe I'm not really out here wandering all alone. Maybe my Father is there, standing and watching. Waiting. Protecting.

Mean Things Your Body May Do
After Breaking Up

1. Memory Loss. Lately I can't remember anything. I can't remember the names of people I've known for years. I can't remember names of songs, but I can recite all the lyrics. I can't remember the name of a restaurant where I've eaten dozens of times. I can't remember. I feel as though I've always had a pretty good memory. Sure, I tend to embellish stories and inflate minor details—but that's all for the benefit of the listener. I've never felt like I just could not remember. Until recently—meaning post-breakup—and recently I can't remember. I feel as if there's an invisible wall in my brain and certain events and facts have chosen to hide behind it. I feel like shouting—come out! I know they're there, just can't see them.

2. The Eyelid Twitch. My eye is twitching. And not every now and then, but all day. Twitching to the point that the room jumps and I start to feel dizzy. It drives me nuts. Stop twitching! I've eaten bananas, gotten more rest, put a cold compress on it and taken vitamins. Still twitching. Whenever I get upset about something (like the nonstop twitching) the other eye starts to twitch. And when they both twitch, it's complete vertigo. I can think of little else but the infernal twitching. It's like having eternal silent hiccups. At first I don't really notice, but after a few minutes it starts to become annoying. After more minutes it becomes aggravating. After even more minutes it becomes a thorn in the flesh. I used to be accused of having a sparkle in my eye, and now all I have is vertiginous twitching.

3. Toothache. My teeth hurt. Even when I drink lukewarm water. Even when I'm just sitting at my desk or driving in my car. And it isn't one tooth—it's all of them. Could I have suddenly developed cavities in every tooth? I thought about making an emergency visit to the dreaded dentist, but I'm desperately trying to avoid that. My roommate Karina's hypothesis is that I'm grinding my teeth at night. I went to the giant sporting goods store around the corner from my office and bought a mouth guard for 99¢. Understandably, it's not the best quality, but I was hoping it would do the trick. It's black and doesn't fit in my mouth. But it makes me look tough and cool like a boxer or a hockey player. It also chokes me and tastes bad. Maybe I should go to the dentist.

4. Baldness. Saturday I went to get my hair cut. Nothing glamorous—just a simple trim. I got to my appointment and greeted my hairdresser, who immediately asked about my hair falling out. She noticed from a distance. I sat down in a slump. Hair? Falling out? She noted that my hair seemed remarkably thinner and it was likely due to the current stress in my life. (You think?) She washed my hair and checked for bald spots. Bald spots!? She didn't find any . . . said I have nothing to worry about. Yeah, thanks.

5. Weight Gain. I can eat. A lot. Mexican and Chinese and French fries and ice cream and more Mexican and French fries. What's the deal with size 4s who "lose their appetite" over the tiniest little upset. I break up with my fiancé and suddenly feel as if I'm eating for two. Me and my heartache. This is completely unfair.

6. Insomnia. I can't sleep. All through the day I count the moments until I get to finally sleep, and then I lie in bed awake, still counting moments. I go all week without sleeping and cherish the Saturday morning sleep-in. Then on Saturday I wake up at 6 AM, after also waking up at 3 and 4 AM. This fills me with rage so that I cannot go back to sleep. I'm to the point of slurring I'm so tired. To the point of drifting off into a catatonic state in the middle of a sentence. I see black spots. I hear nonstop ringing. I'm tired. I go to bed tired and I wake up tired and I'm tired all day. I've tried a warm bath, reading, counting backward from sixty, singing myself lullabies. I haven't tried warm milk because that . . . is . . . gross.

7. The Appearance of Temporary Insanity. Maybe I should invent The Breakup Alert Bracelet. Kinda like a Medic Alert bracelet for people with medical problems. Mine would say Breakup Alert. That way, when strangers see my eyes twitching and my hair falling out and I stop talking mid-sentence, they can just look at my bracelet and all will make sense. They'll mumble Poor thing, she just broke up. When a guy with a pacemaker shows his Pacemaker Alert card at the airport, the security guys don't question it. They understand and allow Pacemaker Guy to move on. I'm hoping that if I wore my Breakup Alert Bracelet, strangers would leave me alone and stay out of my business.

CHAPTER **SIX**

Graveclothes

Unfortunately, I remember it vividly. The time when the aforementioned Void got the best of me. Long before I met Ross, I loved another man. A charming and witty and hilarious man. A man who loved Jesus with his whole life and loved life with his whole heart. Jack. When I met Jack, my world shifted. There was something about his manner and his eyes and his smile. He made me feel special, loved. Would wrap his arms around me like no one had before. His arms felt big and warm, like a place to belong. Like home. Everyone at our university knew his name, and he pretended to know theirs. Mr. Popularity. Mr. Friend of All. When Jack and I started hanging out publicly around campus, girls I had never talked to would stop me and congratulate me on being with Jack. Affirm my status by telling me they were jealous.

He had a habit of always saying the exact thing I needed to hear, bragging on me to his friends and his family. It was always enough to keep me around. There were times throughout our relationship that I felt taken advantage of or overlooked. Times when he would simply forget about me. But then he would tell me how much he needed me and how much he loved me. How he would die without me. So I stayed around.

I loved Jack more than I could explain or understand or verbalize. More than my friends thought was healthy. More than I knew at the time. And he loved me too. He did. He just didn't love me the same way. His love for me was more of the friend variety. And that was okay because I knew that someday he would change his mind or God would change his mind. I knew we would be together. So I waited. I waited for him to see me and realize that the world would make sense if we were together.

But after four years, he still hadn't realized. And finally, I told Jack that I could no longer continue to be his cheerleader. I could no longer be the one that was always there for him and supporting him and loving him unconditionally. I told him this because, a week before, he had told me that I wasn't pretty enough to be his wife. I had just asked him why we seemed to be in the same place we started after four years together. I asked him what went through his mind when his friends called me "Mrs. Jack" and teased him about me. Asked him where he saw us going and where we might end up. And just like that, he said it was my exterior. My body. My face. It wasn't enough. Those weren't his exact words, and honestly I can't fully remember his exact words. I've spent years trying to forget them. But what I heard was, *You're not pretty enough for me. I love you, but I don't want to marry you. I want to marry someone prettier.*

It's hard to really describe exactly how that made me

feel. I felt like a stain. Like a hideous sore that people gawk at. Someone that would make a child hide in fear. Made me feel worthless. The man that I had loved for four years thought I wasn't enough. Looking back, I don't know if he meant it. Maybe he was just scared. Maybe he needed an excuse. Or maybe he did mean it. But it doesn't matter if he meant it or not, because to me it was truth. Universal truth. I opened my heart to him and then he threw daggers at it.

After things between us ended, I retreated inward. Jack had become my whole world. My whole existence. Every part of my future had him in it. I had been biding my time until we would be together. No, he never asked me to marry him. Never even said he wanted to marry me. He just said things like, *I can't wait to grow old with you* and *No other woman could ever replace you.* Things like that. I just assumed that he meant marriage and forever. (Wouldn't you?) But he didn't. And that reality was too harsh for me to process. So I ran.

Shortly after this last conversation with Jack, I moved to Nashville all by myself. I thought it might be a good thing to just start over. For no one to know me as his friend but to just know me as me. I thought I would get over him more quickly if no one knew. I was way off.

What transpired next is a tale of woe too long to tell. The short version is that I was engulfed in three years of the darkest darkness I hope I ever know. My three years of hell. Three years of feeling worthless and hideous and unacceptable. And believing myself to be so. Three years of thinking no one could ever love me again. That I could never love anyone else again, or at least I didn't want to. That I had blown my one shot. That all the stories of God's will and things working together for good were just lies that Sunday school teachers told. He was the one person in my life I measured everyone else against, and he said he didn't find me attractive enough. Whatever he said became truth for me. If he felt that I wasn't attractive enough for him, I became unattractive to the world at large.

> I thought that if I was any sort of Christian I could read my Bible and pray every day until the pain subsided.

This proclamation hurt me so deeply that I retreated from life for a while. At first, I tried to "faith" my way out of it. I thought that if I was any sort of Christian I could read my Bible and pray every day until the pain subsided. That didn't work, so I tried the opposite. I considered ending my life. Thought about that for quite some time. Thought that might be the answer. But toward the end, I just resigned to live a life of lack. Lacking anything happy or fulfilling or good.

I didn't tell anyone about the hurt I was carrying around. I kept it all in, even to my friends. They knew some, but they definitely didn't know all. I told them surface things and assured them I was okay. But I wasn't. I was dying inside. But I felt that I could heal myself. I could discreetly take care of my "problem" without people asking questions and involving themselves. I especially didn't want anyone to think that I was weak. All through college I was the "strong" one who had it all together. At least, that was my perception of myself. It was even one of the things Jack said he loved about me. I thought it very important to keep that up. So I went to work every day and smiled at people and did my job and went home.

But inside I was dying. When Jack told me I wasn't pretty enough, it felt like being ripped apart. So there I was, in Nashville, meeting new people as only half a person. No one knew this, of course. But I did. I felt bloodied and wounded and grotesque. But I continued to say hello and shake hands and act interested. When I lost Jack, I felt that I lost the best part of me. After that, I was just wandering around with a big hole right through my middle. I felt like no one could see me—just the hole. Felt like everyone kept looking at the hole and looking right through me, talking about the hole and wondering when it wouldn't be there anymore. In truth, they weren't. In truth, no one had any idea. But the reality I was living in was that I was incomplete without Jack, and everyone knew it. That I would never be a whole person without him. I had found what I thought to be happiness. The forever kind. But forever didn't last.

In the early days after the separation, it wasn't that I thought about him constantly. But the few thoughts I did have were so powerful. Sometimes they ran me over and I would forget where I was or how I got there. How I became an all-alone person. How I lost my reality and woke up in this bad dream that I now found myself living. Life without Jack. I wanted to wake up and for all the world to be right. At least my kind of right. A world where he and I made sense and were good and where we lived happily ever after. A place where I wouldn't lie in bed at night and cry, not always knowing why.

I wondered what would happen if people stopped looking at the hole in me and actually saw me. Me without him. Me all by myself. I feared that everyone would walk away in disinterest. Maybe that's why the hole didn't fade. I would be rattled awake in the middle of the night from a loud voice. Only it wasn't a voice like Samuel heard when God was calling him. It was the voice of my pain reminding me that it was still there. Why is it so easy to fall in love and so impossible to climb out? I felt like I was in the bottom of a well calling out to anyone who would listen. No one was throwing a rope.

> Why is it so easy to fall in love and so impossible to climb out? I felt disillusioned. I wondered if it was better to just be religious than to honestly struggle with my faith.

I think I wanted someone to notice I was losing it without my having to tell them. I wanted someone to offer the answer without having to ask the question. I didn't want anyone to know—but I wanted everyone to help. So I sank deeper and deeper into myself. Into my pain and my fear and my emptiness. I continued to maintain as much I needed. People at work were satisfied that I was a normal girl. My friends felt that I was back to normal. My family worried but accepted my assurances that I was fine.

But I wasn't. And I knew it. Things of God were slowly losing meaning for me. Things of life were slowly losing meaning for me. I felt disillusioned. I believed in forever, believed I would see Jesus face to face someday. I believed I would one day feel His embrace. I believed that more than I believed anything else but began to think that what I believed might not be enough. It wasn't that I was going through the motions—I felt motionless. Friends around me would talk about prayer and God and change and praises and requests. I would roll my eyes. In meetings at work there would always be a time for prayer requests. To me, it felt fake. I would slide down in my chair so I wouldn't be seen. So I wouldn't be called on to fake-pray for fake prayer requests.

I wondered if maybe I just wasn't spiritual enough. Wondered if it was better to fake-pray than to not pray at all. Wondered if it was better to just be religious than to honestly struggle with my faith. I felt frustrated and angry. I wanted to grab someone, anyone, and shake them by their shoulders until the truth fell out. I hadn't had a real conversation about my faith in a long time. And I felt stagnant. Like there was mold growing in my heart because of inactivity. Nothing bad. Nothing good. Just nothing.

I became less sad, more dead on the inside. I didn't understand this—since Christ lived in me, shouldn't I be able to withstand? Shouldn't I triumph? Shouldn't I be brave and courageous? How could such a thing as losing someone I never really had destroy my life? I wondered where the stories were of Christians who failed. Who couldn't pray. Who felt dead. I thought I must be the only one. Every day would end and I would wonder why it even mattered. And it seemed endless. I still hadn't heard from God. I still missed Jack. I had stopped caring about every single thing. I just couldn't seem to figure out what it all meant. Couldn't figure out where God was. But there was a definite feeling. A certain hanging sense of dread. What else was there? Nothing, I decided, as I sat one night in my bedroom with a handful of pills and a decision to make.

Now a man named Lazarus was sick. (John 11:1)

Lazarus was a friend of Jesus. Can you imagine? A friend of the guy at the top of the rumor mill. Friend of the One who turned water into wine to help out at a friend's wedding. The One who made the blind guy see and forgave the woman caught in bed with a man who wasn't her husband. This man Jesus was going around from town to town causing quite a stir. And Lazarus and his two sisters, Mary and Martha, were His friends. Jesus often stayed with these friends when He was in town. Maybe after dinner they would sit around telling stories and laughing together. Hanging out. And now Lazarus, friend of Jesus, is sick. Mary and Martha sent word to their friend that their brother was sick. To hurry. To help. They were desperate and worried. But they were friends with the one Man who could help. There were, no doubt, many who called for Him; many who wished Jesus would stop by and fix what ailed them. But Mary and Martha were sure He would come. This was Lazarus who was sick. Friend of Jesus.

Yet when he heard that Lazarus was sick,
he stayed where he was two more days. (John 11:6)

Wait. He didn't run? He didn't drop everything? He lingered? How could He do this? How could He abandon His friend? Mary and Martha must have freaked. Where is He? Where IS He? Did He get the message? Has He lost His mind? Did something happen? Were we wrong about Him?

Finally, Jesus arrives—but Lazarus is already dead. In fact, he had already been in the tomb for four days. Sealed. Dead. Martha ran out to meet Jesus, exclaiming that had He come sooner, Lazarus might have lived! When Mary saw Jesus she cried that if only He had been there her brother wouldn't be dead! It could have been so easy. Jesus had done many wonders in the past. Multitudes had seen Him perform miracles. But what about this time? Does He have no feelings? Has He forgotten His friendship? How could this have happened? Now it's too late. He must not be the Man they thought He was.

I don't really remember what sparked it. I don't think there was an incident or a comment or any sort of catalyst. I think I was just tired. Tired in my bones. Way too tired of being so sad, empty, and dried up. It had been three years and I could no longer deal with the pain. The emptiness. Jack, the first man I ever really loved, had broken my heart. Smashed it, to be exact. And I didn't care about life anymore. Didn't care at all. It wasn't a violent thing or a rash, dramatic thing. I was very calm and resolute. It was simply time.

I'm fairly allergic to any over-the-counter medication. Sometimes it makes me break out in hives and these hives can cause my throat to swell shut. (Obviously, not a good thing.) But on this particular night I was okay with that. I thought it might be the easiest thing to do. So I went through my roommate Nivah's bathroom and found all her medicines. She just had typical pain medication and some cold and flu pills and maybe a few aspirin. I decided that would be enough.

I took the medicine back to my room and lined it up on my dresser. It was Friday night, and Nivah would be gone until Monday. I hadn't really made any friends in Nashville, so no one would look for me until I didn't show up for work on Monday morning. Should be pretty easy. I didn't write a letter or anything like that. It wasn't really any sort of attempt at attention. I just wanted to rest. Really rest. No more sleepless nights and no more nightmares and no more memories. I just wanted to sleep. I don't even think I considered what I was doing was permanent. I just wanted to sleep. For a really, really long time.

It all sounds morbid, but I sat for a long time and stared at those bottles of pills. And I thought about every single person in my life—from the important people to mere aquaintances. I thought about what my parents would do when they found out. Probably freak out since they had no idea things had gotten so bad for me. But in time, they would be okay. Thought about what my boss would do. Probably tell the staff about the "tragedy" and then hire someone to replace me. Thought about Nivah. I wondered if our apartment complex would go easy on her about the rent since there had been an accident. Thought about my college roommates Beth and Ape and Laura. They might be mad at me for a while for not telling them sooner. For telling them that I was fine when I wasn't. For telling them the truth in this way. But they were strong women. I knew they would get over it. Maybe it would give them a good story to tell their friends. I knew a girl once who . . . that sort of thing. Thought about Jack. Thought about him a lot. About how he would hear the news and that he might cry. About how this would finally make him see me. About how he would finally understand how much I loved him.

With each person I could fully envision them being okay with it. Relieved, even. (Obviously, I wasn't exactly thinking clearly.) I thought they might be sad for a day or two, but then pictured them saying things like, *Now she's in a better place*, or *At least now she can rest*. I even thought I might be doing them all a favor. Then I thought about my brother, Drew. At the time he was eighteen and a senior in high school. He was wildly popular and smart and charming. He was a star athlete and quite possibly the funniest guy ever. I tried to envision his reaction to the news and it made me sick to my stomach. Drew is strong and brave and grounded.

But I just couldn't shake the feeling that doing this would be cruel to him. Even in that state, I could never intentionally hurt him. I felt it would be too horrible from him to endure—and that would be all my fault. I kept hearing myself say that this would ruin his life.

> I felt like God couldn't hear me anymore, or at least didn't want to. Felt like I was too unimportant and invisible for Him to care.

It's not that I loved any of the others any less, I just somehow felt that they could handle it. I don't know why. And it doesn't matter. But I just wanted to end the pain. Cure the ache. Salve the wound. I felt like I had reached a breaking point and this was my only way out. I felt like God couldn't hear me anymore, or at least didn't want to. Felt like I was too unimportant and invisible for Him to care.

Jesus wept. (John 11:35)

Visibly moved, Jesus wept. He wept over the loss of His friend. He wept over the sorrow of Mary and Martha. Jesus wept. After all He had done, they still didn't believe. Did they still not know Him? Jesus went to the tomb where the body of His friend lay. A tomb. A large cave with an even larger stone sealing the entrance. And He asked some of the men to take the stone away. The gasps were surely audible. Take the stone away? It's really heavy! Lazarus has been in there four days! He's dead! It will . . . smell. But Jesus must have had powerful authority in His voice because they obeyed. Any onlooker who doubted before must now be thinking Jesus to be a mad man. What's the point of this show? What's He trying to prove? And then Jesus asked Lazarus His friend, a man who had been sealed in a tomb for four days, to come out.

The dead man came out. (John 11:44)

One again, the gasps were surely audible. Wrapped in his graveclothes, Lazarus came out—alive! I wonder how the people felt about their doubts. I wonder if their minds were changed. I wonder what they said. What they thought. I wonder if they were speechless. I wonder what expression was on the face of Jesus. The Bible goes on to say that many believed that day—and many also continued to doubt who Jesus was. But there's something else. Something more that Jesus said:

Take off the grave clothes and let him go. (John 11:44)

I was sick. I was broken. I was on the verge of emotional death, crying out to be saved. Hurry! I might not last! But He didn't hurry—and I began to doubt, thinking maybe He didn't love me after all. I thought maybe there were others that were more important to Him. Maybe He didn't get the message. Maybe I was wrong about Him. And I got worse. My heart became diseased and broken, wrapped in graveclothes. I shut myself up in a tomb and threw away the key. At least it was quiet in the tomb. There was no one to bother me about living. In there I could be alone, wrapped in my graveclothes, dying quietly. Besides, it wasn't so bad. It was warm. I had anger and frustration wrapped around my left arm. Loneliness and confusion wrapped around my right. Apathy and disinterest covered my face. Complacency and invisibility were covering my legs and hurt—hurt covered my whole body. I accepted my graveclothes and learned to be comfortable in them. Without them, I felt naked. Exposed. I feared that people might see the real me. It was safer in there, wrapped up tight, behind the big stone. But I heard Him calling me out. I heard Jesus saying with authority for the stone to be moved—and it scared me. I had been in there a long time and wasn't sure I was ready to leave. But He called me out.

Hours later I found myself still sitting there with the pills still lined up on my dresser. Still numb. Still empty. But alive. I'm sure God used the thought of my brother to help me out. Because at that moment, Drew was my one and only reason for living. My one reason to stick around. It wasn't some light-bulb moment. Everything didn't get better after that night. I just decided to keep going.

> Sometimes healing must take place one layer at a time.

And that's how it was for me. Jesus called me out and I resisted. I wanted to stay in the safety of my tomb and rest. I was afraid and scared. But He was still there, in the quiet. In the dark. So when Ross and I broke up, I remembered back to this time of my life. The time when I gave up all hope of ever feeling normal again. Of ever feeling loved again.

When I lost Ross, I didn't feel as if all life had ended. I had already learned where my value truly lies. I knew that God was big enough and strong enough to see me through the worst. I knew that losing Ross didn't mean I had lost the best part of me. Because Ross isn't the one who completes me. And I know God is there and He is the One who makes me whole and restores me. I know that when I think He's lingering far away, He knows exactly where I am. He hasn't forgotten me or abandoned me, even though I may feel as if He has.

It's hard when you try to face the daylight after being in the dark for so long. The graveclothes don't instantly fall away. But I've found that they tend to unravel the less that I need them. And I can see the sunlight one layer at a time. I can feel the fresh air and the cool breeze of life. When Jesus calls us out, it's not always in an instant. Sometimes it's after we've given up hope. When we think too much time has passed and He must not care. Sometime we've wrapped ourselves in graveclothes so tight, it's hard to hear His call. Sometimes healing must take place one layer at a time.

Top Ten Things My Friends Did Immediately After Breaking Up

✦ I screamed at Brian in the middle of a restaurant. We both worked there and he was my supervisor. He was bullying me and wouldn't let me take a break so I screamed at him in front of everyone. —Jen

✦ James bought me a stuffed bunny when I was in the hospital. After we broke up, I cut the ears off the bunny. —Katherine

✦ I overfertilized his lawn so that he had to cut it four times a week. —Amy

✦ I mailed all of our pictures to his new girlfriend's mom. —Andrea

✦ I took the money from our ring fund (we had been saving for an engagement ring together) and bought several pairs of really, really expensive shoes. —Tiffany

✦ I enrolled in a sculpting class and made a bust of Jason. Then I smashed it. —Beth

Graveclothes

✦ I got a carton of eggs and wrote on each egg one of the awful things he said to me when we broke up. Then my friend Julie and I went to the edge of a cliff and I threw them off. This is called Egg Therapy. You should try it. —Susan

✦ I dated his brother. —Laurie

✦ My friend Erica and I would write e-mails to each other that we really wanted to send to our ex-boyfriends. Then this other weird girl found the e-mails and sent them to the boys!!! AHHHHHHHHHHHH!!! —Claudia

CHAPTER **SEVEN**

The New Me

Was there ever a time when airlines wouldn't allow you to carry on your own luggage? I love carrying on. Well, sorta. I don't like waiting in line to get on the plane because someone at the front of the line is taking their precious time putting their carry-on in the overhead bin. I don't like it when it's time to get off the plane and people fumble with their bags, holding up the already impatient line of people waiting to get off and get on with life. (I also despise when people jump up to rush off when we all are in the back of the plane and there won't be any leaving anytime soon and they will just have to half-stand with their heads crammed under the overhead bin waiting and sighing and grunting—I hate that. Please calm down.)

I also don't like the part about dragging my carry-on all the way to the very last gate in the terminal, which seems to always be my gate. Luggage (especially mine) tends to be too heavy and too bulky. I'd much rather have only a purse and a certain sashay about me appearing glamorous and breezy. Lugging luggage while trying to use the ladies' room has a certain lack of grace. I'd rather sip my Diet Coke and frolic to the gate with ease. Look at me! World traveler! Not a care in the world!

Today my friend Joni busted into the service at church during the announcements carrying five suitcases and a scowl. The suitcases weren't cooperating as she tried to make it to the stage. She shoved and pushed. Growled and heave-ho'd. As I suspected, she was performing a skit about carrying around your past like heavy baggage. She lugged the luggage onstage and shouted at God about how heavy they all were and how much trouble it was to carry them all around all the time. Then Pete, my pastor, put several huge, heavy stones in a backpack and struggled to put it on. It was so heavy it nearly threw him backward. He wore the cumbersome backpack while talking about carrying around a grudge and how heavy that can be. *Hmmm*, I thought. *What are You trying to tell me, God?*

I remember how long it took me to get rid of the baggage from my relationship with Jack. I carried that hurt around in plain view for, well, years. Three years, actually. I'm not proud of this fact. But, it cannot be denied. This hurt, this injustice, became my identity. I carried it around with me everywhere I went and just became more and more bent over from the weight. Every new person I met would be mentally put through the hurt filter. Will this person hurt me too? Will they understand how fragile I am? Truth is, most people didn't seem to care who I was or what I'd been through, which I immediately chalked up to another injustice to my already heavy grudge. Woe is me, I thought. No one could ever love me. And that's true. Who would want to love a bent-over, bitter grudge transporter?

I move every year. I've now lived in Nashville for a little more than six years and tomorrow I'm moving to my seventh address. If you count my short stint in Boston, it's my eighth. No particular reason why I do this; there just has always been some reason to move—like cheaper rent or proximity to work or boredom. The good thing about moving so often is that I've sufficiently rid myself of the useless things that tend to hang around, except for those few stragglers that have some sort of significance. Like my Ross Box. I went through it yesterday and actually threw some things out. Like the stuffed moose he gave me and a plaque bearing the meanings of both our names and our wedding date. I also threw out the matching sweatshirts my parents gave us (those weren't so hard to part with), but I kept the pictures and his letters and a journal I had written to him. I kept an "Our First Christmas" ornament that's inscribed with "We Belong Together. Ross and JoAnna." Moving would have been the perfect opportunity to throw these things out. To rid myself of the tangible memories. But I kept them, and I don't know why.

Sometimes, holding on to the past can become an identity. I remember my third day at my current job, which was also my third year apart from Jack. I had finally gotten my life back together somewhat. Started a new job. Gotten involved in a church. Found things to be happy about. The dark places in my heart, although present, weren't so dark anymore. And I was happy about that. I went to lunch with the new girls from my new job and conversation turned (as usual with girls) to relationships. Past, present, and future. For some reason, girls tend to get to the nitty-gritty fairly quickly with each other. I wonder if guys do this. I wonder if on the third day of knowing someone they would talk about past relationships and what happened to them. Somehow I doubt it.

The new girls asked me about my past and if there was anything interesting in it. I said that I had loved someone for too long and then it ended and that it was a bad thing. I didn't give away many details, trying to sound interesting without giving too much away. I didn't want to scare them off with my sad tale of love lost. These girls didn't know me, and I wanted to put my best foot forward. I was hoping we would be friends as well as coworkers. They asked me what happened to this character from my past and I told them where he worked and about the girl he was engaged to marry. Surprisingly, my new coworker said his name. First and last. "Are you talking about Jack Jennet?"

Hearing his name come out of this virtual stranger so suddenly and casually was an incomprehensible astonishment that knocked the wind out of me. My new coworker, a girl I had known for only three days, said his name just like that. Turns out she had a friend who knew him. Who *knew* him. Who, in fact, became the *new* JoAnna after Jack and I went our separate ways. Who did all the same things with Jack that I had and felt all the same things I had. Who heard the same things from Jack that I did and felt the same hurt. I don't want to call her my replacement because I feel that she deserves more than that, but I think that for Jack, she was. He filled in the empty spot next to him, the spot that once belonged to me, with someone new. The new me.

About two weeks after I saw Jack for the last time, he began a new relationship with this replacement girl. A relationship exactly like the one we had! From what I'm told, he told her the same things he told me—word for word. He took me home to meet his parents. He took her home to meet his parents. He told me I was unlike any woman he had ever met. He told her she was unlike any woman he had ever met. He asked me to help him in ministry. He asked her to help him in ministry. He asked me to lead a small group of girls. He asked her to lead a small group of girls. He told me I wasn't pretty enough. He told her she wasn't pretty enough. Then he asked another girl in her small group to marry him.

> I had been carrying a heavy, heavy load. After all those years and all the pain and hurt and guilt—I realized the truth in an instant.

That day after lunch with the girls, I was driving home thinking about everything I had learned. About how he replaced me with someone new, and how she must have gone through the same horror that I had. I thought about how unfair it all was and how shocking it was that he would do that to her. I knew who this girl was and she was fabulous in every way. Beautiful and talented and smart and . . . that's when it hit me. Struck me. Blindsided me. It wasn't me. It was him. After all those years and all the pain and hurt and guilt—I realized the truth in an instant. I was driving down Hillsboro Road and nearly crashed my car.

I remember calling my friend Nivah that day and shouting that I got it. I finally got it! It wasn't me! He's the crazy one! I am enough! I am enough! And until that moment, I had been carrying a heavy, heavy load. For years I had been stooped over, feeling that I wasn't enough. That nothing about who I was would ever be enough for anyone. That I had lost the closest thing to true love that I would ever find. I had some heavy stones in my backpack. Stones of memories and hurt feelings and what-ifs. Stones of a misrepresented identity. I had become the woman left behind. The woman he didn't love. The heartbroken.

I was holding a grudge against myself—for not measuring up. For not being the woman Jack wanted. For being me and not someone else.

Grudge. Rhymes with sludge. The stuff that slows you down. Something like muck and mire. The yuck. The bad stuff. Stuff to avoid. I wonder if it's coincidence that grudge and sludge sound so similar. I wonder if I believe in coincidence. Not that I think rhyming words have some spiritual significance, but maybe they could. Maybe when I think about holding a grudge—carrying the baggage of it—I should think about sludge. Maybe I should remember that it's only going to slow me down and make me tired and smell kinda funny.

Being freed from the emotional baggage of self-doubt made me a new person. Taller and happier and . . . myself. Sometimes giving up the hurt, the injustices from others, is the hardest thing to give up. The past becomes a name tag. Hi, I'm JoAnna-and-the-Only-Man-I-Ever-Loved-Thought-I-Wasn't-Enough. But the past doesn't have to own me. I am not the woman Jack told me I was. I am the woman God created.

The hardest part about carrying around the past is that it's usually more than one issue, more than one grudge to bear. It's true that I had an epiphany that Jack's opinion of me wasn't truth, but that fact didn't entirely erase him from my heart.

I remember once missing Jack so incredibly that I called his voice mail at work, just to hear his voice. This was several years after we'd parted ways. It's humiliating to admit, but I did it. Years after I should have forgotten about him. I wanted to move on . . . and I had. But I kept discovering new parts of me—small tiny hidden parts—that hadn't forgotten him. Like a bad habit. One of those habits that you know you should quit but you enjoy so you don't. But I did! I walked away! Somehow parts of me were unaware of that. There was a corner of my heart still waiting for things to start up again. For him to be with me and for everything to go back to the wonderful way it . . . wasn't. It wasn't wonderful. I was in a battle with myself over how to write the past. One of us was lying, but who?

I couldn't believe I called him.

I worried that someone might find out. That I was alone

in my backward desperation. The Israelites did it too. Longed for a past that wasn't worth longing for. Wished to be back in the comfort of the known. Egypt meant slavery—but Egypt was home. The desert was freedom—but challenging and frightening and unknown. The unknown can appear to be worse than the known, no matter how bad the known is. What we know is what we understand. What defines us—makes us feel comfortable. But how can we be comfortable with mediocre? Second best. Bad, even. I was no different. I longed for the embrace of a man who didn't love me back. Crazy, but true. Because it's still an embrace.

I couldn't believe I called him.

I wanted to know what the sound of his voice would do to me after three years. I called late so he wouldn't be there and I could hear his voice mail. I can't even write it, it's so mortifying. He probably never had one single thought about me, and I was stalking him through voice mail. I wanted to believe he hadn't moved on either. Wanted to believe that he thought of me daily and contemplated calling me but was afraid. If anyone else were telling this story I would shake my head and wonder what her problem was. But I can't shake my head. It's me. I'm the troubled one.

The sound of his voice still made my heart skip a beat. What was it about him that I couldn't seem to shake? I felt like God wasn't answering my prayers, at least not in the way I wanted Him to. I kept thinking I was making it to the other side only to find another bend in the road. I wondered if I was the only woman alive who held on that long to an invisible love. Then one week later, God answered in a way I couldn't have imagined.

Seems like my whole life has been about small groups and Bible studies and youth groups. Even during the dark days. Sometimes I think I've heard it all. In my adult life, it's rare that I've attended a class or event and felt that I've really gotten something new or challenging. It's not that I'm Captain Christian. Just tired. And sometimes jaded, I'll admit. I do believe that Scripture is constantly fresh and forever new, it's the surrounding church activities I have a problem with.

Toward the end of the three-year darkness, I began attending a new church. It was the first church I had attended in those three years that seemed to have something to say. That seemed genuine. But, when I was asked to be a small-group leader for the women's ministry, I sighed *Yes* and knew I was signing on for another yawn. The class was fifteen weeks long. Quite a commitment. The information was great, though. Many women learned vital truths that actually changed their lives. But for me, not so much. It was good to be a part. Good to see God move in others' lives. Good to know that sometimes things like classes at church actually work.

Much of the class was about discovering things in your past, facing them, and dealing with them. About understanding sin and forgiveness. The last class was to be a "burning ceremony." Women were instructed to make a list of things to forgive or forget. Things that still had a hold on them that needed burning. There would be an actual fire and women would be able to burn their lists. (Sounds like a sappy, contrived youth camp event, right?) I knew I would need to attend since I was a leader, but of course I wouldn't participate. I had already survived the darkest moments possible. There couldn't be anything left for me to deal with or reconcile. I spoke to the women in my group and made sure they understood. They did. Then I went on my merry way thinking of friends to see and things to do. Women who had taken the class before talked all about how amazing and incredible the final class would be. That sounded nice, but it wasn't for me. I was the leader. The teacher. I already had my stuff figured out. Sure, I had just called Jack a week earlier in some crazy attempt to relive the past, but I didn't need to do anything drastic like this so-called burning ceremony.

The event was taking place on a Saturday morning. (*I have to get up early? Humph.*) The night before the list burning I watched a movie with some friends, had some laughs, and went home. As I was walking up the stairs of my apartment I was literally knocked over by an overwhelming feeling that I had things to burn. Things to purge. Things that were rotting in my apartment and in my mind. Up until that point, I thought myself to be "above" this exercise. I was, after all, a leader. A teacher. I had all my issues worked out, right? No. I didn't.

It was late and the event was early the next morning. I stayed up half the night searching until I found it all. I went through my entire apartment and gathered everything from him. Every letter, every picture, every journal page I had written about him. Words and memories that were years old and long gone. Most of these things I hadn't looked at in quite some time. Still, it was comforting to me to know that they were there. Because I would read them when I got lonely. I would look at his picture when I felt low. Sometimes it made me feel better. Sometimes worse. Either way, it was time to go. I stayed up all night reading every word and drinking in every picture. Letting go of these things was not exactly my idea of a good time. But I realized that I had been lying to myself. These memories were just that, memories. His promises would never come true, no matter how many times I read them. His picture would always be a smile in the past. This fact sat like a stone inside me, but I knew it was true. Sometimes the teacher must learn herself. I wasn't even sure if I could go through with it. I think I prayed for God to change His mind. Actually, that sounds more righteous than what I really did. The prayers of my heart that night were, *Don't make me! I don't wanna! NO!*

The next morning I gathered my offering and went to the meeting. Little did I know how hard it would be. I got to the meeting and noticed something troubling. I was the only person who had two armfuls of stuff. Everyone else had a neat list folded in her pocket. The point of the burning ceremony was to burn the past. It could be the name of a person you needed to forgive. Could be something from your past that was a regret. Whatever. I seemed to be the only one who had more than a pocketful of regrets. I placed all my items under my chair and tried to act nonchalant. Maybe no one would suspect these were items to burn and I could take it all back home where it belonged. I mean, I was over him.

I was. But does that mean that I have to burn him, too? I think not. It was settled. I was just going to take it all back home. I could always burn it later. God would understand.

"To love is to burn, to be on fire."
Sense and Sensibility, Jane Austen

Things got started and, for me, got worse. A woman would approach the fireplace and throw in her list. The list would linger a moment and then lightly burn down to ashes. (I wondered if my heap would send the blaze out of control.) She might take a moment, might pause to watch it burn, but all in all it was fairly quiet and respectful. Women were burning the names of people who had hurt them, a past relationship she felt she failed, the name of an abuser. I finally decided to approach, all the while screaming *NO!* on the inside. Not fully understanding my attachment to the words, the pictures, the memories, I burst into tears. I threw the pictures in first, upside down so I wouldn't have to see them. (Obedience isn't always the most pleasant of actions.) The one picture I cherished most, the picture from our first date, landed faceup. I watched it burn and felt that I might burst into flames myself. Afraid I might hurl myself into the fireplace to save the picture. To save the memory. To save the girl I used to be. Instead, I watched it burn. Next I threw in his letters. Every written word I had from him. And I wept. Strange— the very things I threw into the fire were the very things I would have run to save in the event of a fire. But I threw them in. It was me telling God that I was ready to give it up. It was me tangibly saying that I believed Jesus was enough. I was serious. That was the end of it. I was burning him out of my life for good.

And I realized a few things. I realized that sometimes people don't turn out the way we thought they would. That the good life we wish we had isn't always better than the life we've got. That following your heart isn't always the best thing to do. Don't gasp—it's true. If I followed my heart, I would still be waiting for him.

> I realized that sometimes people don't turn out the way we thought they would. That following your heart isn't always the best thing to do.

My roommate told me a story she heard from a friend about the refiner's fire. The story goes that when a silversmith is crafting his metal, he holds the metal directly in the flame of the fire until he can see his own reflection in it. That's when he knows it's ready. That's when he knows it's good. Shaped. Strong. Refined. It's a very precise process, this heating and firing. Makes me wonder if that's what's happening in my life. If burning my past brought about a burning of me. Burning away the old. The bad. Making me shaped and strong. Refined. The last part of the story is that the silversmith cannot take his eyes off the metal until it's exactly ready. If he looks away, even for a moment, the metal could be ruined. He must keep his eyes firmly planted on the metal until he can see his reflection.

Some say that the hard times either break you or make you stronger. I think it's both. I think they're the same thing. Isaiah 48:10 says that God refines us, but not as silver. He tests us in the furnace of affliction. Wow. Sounds harsh at first, but I think it's actually quite good. Life is life. Things happen, things that afflict and hurt and cause us pain. This refining process isn't always easy. God uses these afflictions, these hurts, to shape our hearts. But I trust Him. Even when things don't make sense and seem too heavy to endure. He uses circumstances to grow us. To grow me. I wonder if God can see His reflection in me yet.

CHAPTER **EIGHT**

Friends Who Carried Me

I've had some realizations lately. Like that I haven't had a cold or the flu in exactly one year. I realized I haven't worn shoes with a heel in over two, maybe three years. Apparently I can't be bothered with a shoe that I can't just slide my foot into. No-Hassle Girl, that's me. I realized that I've finally reached an age when younger people are smarter than me and could become my boss. I realized that the older I get the smaller the world gets, history really does repeat itself, and I will never ever use calculus. I also realized the immeasurable value of old friends.

And by old friends, I mean the true kind. The kind of friends that have been around the block with me, more than once, and would choose to go around again. Friends that have no secrets and no restrictions and no limit of love to give. My friends have seen the best in me—and the worst. Oddly enough, none of them have run screaming or sighed a disinterested yawn. Or worse, none of them have cut me off. Shut me out. They just love me over and over and over in spite of myself.

I flew to Tampa this weekend to visit my old friend Leigh Ann; I'm happy this is becoming a yearly jaunt. At the airport, Leigh Ann welcomed me by hanging out of the sunroof of her SUV, hollering and waving a sign that said "Glam JoAnna." The fact that she thought to do this, and knew how much I would love it, is why Leigh Ann is one of my old friends. I met Leigh Ann over ten years ago. She was a Kappa Delta, the sorority I would soon be pledging. She had long curly hair (at that time often worn in a big purple bow) and an infectious laugh with a matching smile. She was the seasoned sophomore while I was still a wide-eyed and eager freshman. I don't remember the exact moment, but somewhere along the way I knew that Leigh Ann would always be my friend. And she has been. She has always been my biggest fan in everything I've tried to do. We even dated the same guy once (at different times of course). She took me on a surprise scavenger hunt for my twenty-first birthday and held me when Jack broke my heart years ago. She taught me what it really means to love Jesus with abandon. Now she lives in Tampa with her dashing husband, Rick, whom she met while they were both in medical school. He's the perfect mate for my old friend. The last time I saw Leigh Ann, I was planning my wedding. We sat by her pool and talked for hours about the wedding and the honeymoon and what to expect. We planned and dreamed. We shopped for Godiva chocolates and wedding gifts for my soon-to-be husband.

This trip was a bit different. The wedding had been called off and plans were canceled. We sat by her pool and talked for hours about how to keep going when the world seems to stop and what to do when the future changes in a moment. We shopped for shoes and for groceries and spent time together. And even though my life had dramatically changed since the last visit, our friendship hadn't changed a bit. Since Leigh Ann and Rick are both medical doctors, I take whatever they prescribe as the gospel truth. She has helped me through an annoying case of adult acne, my hair falling out, weird pains, and twitching eyelids. This time it was a broken heart.

One of the best parts about me is that I have more than one old friend. Like my friend Laura, who now lives in Boston with her husband, Michael, and understands why putting "naked" at the end of sentences is funny. Who has a New Testament with "Wan" engraved on the front that matches my New Testament with "ted" engraved on the front—because, at the time we engraved them, we were Wanted Women. Who traveled across the world with me, including the smelly Gatwick airport in London with hallways that are entirely too narrow. I remember the day we met. I was twelve, and my family was visiting Woodland Baptist Church. During the greet-your-neighbor time slot in the program, two girls my age rushed over to say hello. I was wearing my powder blue North Side jacket with my name stitched across the back in yellow. Powder blue and yellow were North Side High school colors, and the jackets were all the rage. I was a seventh grader and went to a Christian school, but I had the jacket and therefore was cool. Or so I thought. Pictures seem to tell a different story.

So the girls hurried over, all smiles, extending huge Baptist handshakes and said hello. They were Laura and Robin, sisters, and were so glad I was there. They weren't wearing North Side jackets. I think I might have glanced in their direction and mumbled a disinterested "Hi."

Laura is hilarious and grounded, both at the same time. And she's consistent with her faith and her life. It's one of my favorite things about her. On New Year's Day I was in Boston, not sure how much longer I could survive all alone with a shattered heart. Ross had just walked out the door (which turned out to be the last time I ever saw him) and took with him all the oxygen from the room. I couldn't breathe or think or blink. I called my old friend Laura to tell her that my life was falling apart. She said don't worry, just come to my house and I'll take care of you. And she did— in a way I couldn't have possibly asked for or known that I needed. I'm fairly certain I would have fallen clear off the deepest deep end if she hadn't been there at that pivotal moment. My mother says that God moved Laura and her husband close to Boston just for me. I don't think God's plan centers that acutely around me, but I'm glad they were there anyway.

And Nivah. I met Nivah about the same time I met Leigh Ann. Nivah and I were both freshmen and both pledged Kappa Delta sorority. A year after college I was living in Louisville and Nivah was living in Chicago. We both moved to Nashville at the same time and became roommates. I lived with Nivah for two hilarious years. We both had long-distance boyfriends for awhile, and I was there when hers broke her heart. I was also there when she met the man she eventually married. Nivah forced me to go to a singles function at a new church, which turned out to be okay since we both met boys that night. (Note: My crush lasted five days. She married hers.) I was there when she said "I do" to the greatest guy, and I hope to be there when her first baby enters this world. More than anyone else I know, Nivah has a deeply spiritual faith. Not like a New Age crystal pusher, but deeply spiritual. Her love for Jesus is rich and wide and real. I admire her enormously and am honored to be her friend. She has the kind of spirit that lifts you off the ground. That makes you believe you can accomplish your goals. You can run another half mile. You can say no to another slice of pizza. You can recover. You can go on. You can learn to breathe in and out again. When Ross and I broke up, Nivah flew to Boston to bring me home.

I called Nivah the night Ross and I broke up. I knew she would be mailing out invitations for a wedding shower the next day, so I called to tell her not to bother. I don't remember what we said to each other, but I remember her telling me that she would come get me. That I wouldn't have to drive back to Tennessee by myself. That may have been what got me through the night.

Then there's Beth, whom I met a few days before we both entered the seventh grade at a brand-new Christian school. Our parents were two of the four couples that started the school. We've been friends every single day since. Through the awkward seventh-grade matching-teddy-bear-sweater-school-picture incident (which we thought was *sooo* cool at the time). Through starting college and growing up. Through discovering how much we liked boys and discovering how much we didn't. We were roommates throughout college and now both live in Nashville. She married Gary, her date to our first sorority formal. She loves cheese. And out of every friend I've ever had in my life, Beth is the one friend I've never argued with. Sure, I've aggravated her and provoked her, but she's always just rolled her eyes and loved me in spite of it. When I turned twenty-nine she gave me a birthday cake that had Fourth of July sparklers as candles. That's Beth. She's the smartest person I know, literally. And so incredibly creative. And like Laura, is consistent. Her faith seems to only grow, never fade. She's the friend who doesn't go around talking about her love for God, but it's always evident at the exact right moment. The one who always says the perfectly wise and incredible thing just in time.

And then there's April, who will forever be Ape to me. (No, she is not hairy or resembling a monkey in any way.) Ape and I met in college when she pledged Kappa Delta. Later, she moved in with me and Laura and Beth. She made us laugh with her oddities like eating gummy sharks and drinking Squirt and made us mad when she turned every guy's head in the cafeteria without even knowing it. She would skip out of her room every day and ask me and Beth and Laura if she looked cute. We usually looked haggard and were still wearing yesterday's T-shirt, so we never thought her cute question was very cute. Because she did always look cute. She married The Colonel (whose name is Lee) and became a financial analyst. I don't even know what that means. Like the rest, the one thing I most admire about Ape is her faith. You could bounce a quarter off her faith. In all the years I've known her, and in all the trying times and unsteady times and frustrating times and scary times, she's never faltered. She's one of those that when the smoke clears, her faith stands. Oh yeah, and she's currently the treasurer of her couples Sunday school class. That makes me laugh.

I asked Laura to call Beth and Ape and let them know about the wedding cancellation. I had told Laura and Nivah and my parents, and I just couldn't tell it again. Couldn't say the words again. Couldn't hear the shock on the other end of the line again. A few months later I got together with Beth and Ape and told the story. Spilled my guts. And they listened and sighed and understood. Beth and Ape both have a quiet nature that's a good balance for my overactive personality. (Read: loud and obnoxious.) Being with them those months later was comforting and soothing. Kinda like being with . . . well . . . an old friend. Friends who understand without demands or questions or selfish motives. So many people had been bombarding me with curiosities and inquiries that I was on the verge of a volatile episode. But not Beth and Ape. They were patient and thoughtful of exactly what I needed—which was time. All of these amazing women are friends that I need and love.

One commonality among these friends is that they all are married. In fact, I was a bridesmaid in each one of their weddings. My five friends all seem to live seamless cookie-cutter lives. I realize that they don't, actually, but to a single girl like myself whose life is a series of mountaintop highs and death valley despairs with nothing in between—they seem fairly level. They seem to have it all together. Several of them have earned graduate degrees and beyond, some have done mission work, and some have bought their first homes. Some of them are thinking of starting families and some have a baby on the way. Sometimes I feel like the only failure. We had always dreamed of the husband and the house and the baby. Talked about who would go first. Oddly enough, I was the one usually chosen as First to Get Married. But we grew up. Our lives have all shifted and changed in ways we couldn't have imagined. Especially me. The black sheep. Their single friend.

It was these five women that I chose to be bridesmaids in my wedding. These women were the people I wanted standing beside me when I vowed my life to the man I loved. Women whom I admire and look up to and love. Women who honor their husbands and love their friends and follow their God with their lives. And it was these women who held me up when I thought I would fall apart.

These five friends have all seen the worst parts of me and choose to love me still. Maybe even a little more. They could care less if I'm married or single or rich or poor or short or tall. They don't love me for who I was supposed to be. They love me for who I am. Sure, I would like to be married someday and share that part of life with them. But for now, I know that I'm blessed beyond anything I deserve. There's nothing I have done or could ever do that would make me deserving of these women. Because of them, I am a better person. Because of them, I have survived. Because of them, I know Christ more. The director of women's ministry at my church often talks to us about being Jesus with skin on. That is what these five friends have been to me.

> When I think that God has abandoned me and given up on me, I hope I will have the wherewithal to remember His most creative gift to me. My friends.

I hope that in as much as I've taken from these friends I've somehow managed to give some, too. Having friends, friends like these, was part of my survival. Sometimes I felt like they *were* my survival. During the dark days when I couldn't see one foot into the future, they believed in me. Days when I couldn't pray, they prayed for me. Days when I wasn't sure if God existed or cared anymore, they knew that He did and lived as if He did. These five women have never, *never* given up on me. And they have had plenty of chances and more than enough reasons. I'm a high-maintenance friend. I tend to get my heart broken a lot. Chances are, I'll get my heart broken again in the future. And they will be there. They were there for me the first time. And the second. So no matter what heart-wrenching situation I find myself in, they will love me and pray for me and listen to me and pray for me some more. Even when I don't want them to. Even when I scream that it doesn't work. When I give up, they'll keep on. I think, I hope, that if I find myself in another desert of loneliness—when I think that God has abandoned me and given up on me—I hope I will have the wherewithal to remember His most creative gift to me. My friends. He knew how much I would need them. Knows how much I need them still. Because of them, I am not alone.

Community seems to be a church buzzword these days. I go to a *community* church and we talk a lot about the importance of *community* and creating *community* and participating in *community*. Which is a good thing—as long as we're all talking about *real* community. I think sometimes you can say a word so many times that you forget what it means. Kinda like the word *love*. How is it possible that I can *love* to wear jeans and *love* to eat ice cream and *love* my brother. I think we've sorta done the same thing with community.

We need *real* community. Not boxes of clothes and canned goods. We need conversation. Eye contact. Touch. Boxes of clothes and canned goods are good and necessary things, but we need friends to listen and love and be there. When Ross and I broke up, I needed community. Real community. My friends saw that need and came to my rescue. And not just the five women I've talked about, but AJ and Karina and Kim and Tiffany and Englert and Heather and Jennifer and Monica and Breeon and Nicole and Laura. These women called me and wrote me letters and had lunch with me and made sure I knew that I wasn't alone.

Made sure that I knew I was loved. I'm a rich woman, because of real community in my life.

> We need real community. Not boxes of clothes and canned goods.

I learned the importance of community a few years ago. When Jack broke my heart, I cut myself off from everything and everyone. I was so defeated and hopeless—and I didn't want anyone to know it. I wanted to appear strong and resilient. I thought that's what a good Christian should do. I thought that someone with faith in Christ could overcome any obstacle. What I didn't realize was that I needed my friends. I needed support. I needed people who could talk to God when I couldn't. Who loved me unselfishly.

One of my favorite stories in the Bible is the story of the Paralyzed Guy (and that's what I'll call him since he is unnamed in the Bible):

A few days later, when Jesus again entered Capernaum, the people heard that he had come home. So many gathered that there was no room left, not even outside the door, and he preached the word to them. Some men came, bringing to him a paralytic, carried by four of them. (Mark 2:1–3)

At this point, Jesus had become quite the popular guy among the Average Joe population. Wherever Jesus went, people gathered. Like a celebrity of the moment. Everyone wanted to know what He would say next. What He would do. Since there was no media or television or high-speed Internet, people had to show up and hear Him and see Him in person. This particular day, Jesus arrived in Capernaum and the crowds ascended.

Down the street were five friends sitting around, maybe looking for something to do. One of the guys was paralyzed. He would lie all day on a mat on the floor and stare at the ceiling. Maybe he had a good personality or maybe he was funny—because he had four good friends. On this day, one of the friends must have heard that Jesus was in town. Maybe one of the guys told a story he had heard around town about this Jesus guy healing a leper.

"Hey, let's take Paralyzed Guy over to Jesus and see if He can heal him."

"Sure, sounds like a cool idea."

"Yeah, I'm in. We don't have anything else to do."

I can see Paralyzed Guy lying on his mat on the floor, rolling his eyes. I can hear him telling his friends, "Yeah right. I've heard about this Jesus guy too. I heard that wherever He goes there's a huge crowd. I don't want to be carted around in a huge crowd and stared at. Besides, we don't even know if this guy is for real. I'm paralyzed. Can't walk. Why don't you guys just go and I'll stay here. I'll . . . lie around or something. Don't worry about me. I'm fine right here. You go." I imagine that Paralyzed Guy said all these things while his four friends were picking up his mat and carrying him out the door.

Must have been quite a sight when they got close. Maybe they couldn't even get really close. Trying to balance a paralyzed guy on a mat in a crowd can't be easy. But his friends were determined. They probably pushed themselves farther and farther into the crowd, no doubt making people angry, until they could see the house where Jesus was. I bet Paralyzed Guy looked over and saw the people hanging out the windows and doors trying to see Jesus. Maybe there were even some other people there seeking healing. Maybe this made him feel dumb. "Come on, guys, really. Let's just go. There's too many people; we'll never be able to get in. Maybe Jesus is a big phony anyway. Let's go, please. I'm embarrassed and I'm hungry. Let's GO."

Since they could not get him to Jesus because of the crowd, they made an opening in the roof above Jesus and, after digging through it, lowered the mat the paralyzed man was lying on. (Mark 2:4)

While Paralyzed Guy was whining to leave, I wonder if his four friends looked at one another knowingly. I wonder if the roof was Plan B, or if it was just a spur-of-the-moment idea. In either case, these four friends pushed through the crowd to the side of the house, and carried their friend up to the roof. At that time, houses were built out of stone and had flat roofs made out of mud and straw. There were usually narrow stairways built into the sides of the houses. I'm sure, given the people and the pushing and the shoving, it wasn't easy getting onto the roof. Four guys had to maneuver Paralyzed Guy on his mat through the crowd and up the stairs onto the roof. They must have been determined.

They must have believed in this Jesus guy they had heard about. They must have loved their friend.

Once on the roof, these four friends dug a hole in the roof. I wonder if the homeowner was there. I wonder if a clump of roof-mud fell on his head. I wonder if any mud fell on Jesus. After digging a big enough hole, and surely causing a big scene, the friends lowered their friend to Jesus.

> *When Jesus saw their faith, he said to the paralytic, "Son, your sins are forgiven."* (Mark 2:5)

Wow. Can you imagine? Jesus Christ, Son of God, looking you in the eye and telling you that you're forgiven. Must have been overwhelming. Must have been enough. But there's more . . . some teachers of the law were there and openly challenged Jesus on His statement. They said He couldn't possibly forgive sins—only God could do that! Jesus challenged them right back, asking which would be easier, to forgive the man or to make him walk again?

> *"But that you may know that the Son of Man has authority on earth to forgive sins . . ." He said to the paralytic, "I tell you, get up, take your mat and go home." He got up, took his mat and walked out in full view of them all. This amazed everyone and they praised God, saying, "We have never seen anything like this!"* (Mark 2:10–12)

Paralyzed Guy walked out. Jesus told him to get up and walk and he did. Just like that. I've heard this story all my life, and it's always been a good one. But lately I've thought about it in a different way. What about the four friends? If these four friends hadn't carried their friend to Jesus, he wouldn't have been able to walk home. He'd still be lying on a mat at home, all alone. Sad. Paralyzed. Unable to participate in life the way his friends could. Maybe he was bitter before he met Jesus. Maybe he was angry. Maybe he was depressed. Then one day his friends carried him to Jesus. And his life was never the same after that day.

I've been paralyzed. Paralyzed by despair and sadness and a lack of hope. I've been lying in bed, staring at the ceiling, unable to move. Not wanting to participate in life anymore. Feeling like an outcast. Defective. Sometimes breaking up can make you feel immobile. Like you don't wanna go anywhere or do anything. Like your legs, or your heart, just won't work anymore. That's how I felt. But I had friends who were willing to carry me to Jesus. Friends who believed in His healing power and would withstand any obstacle to get me there. I didn't really wanna go. I didn't want the hassle or the crowds or people to stare at me. But because of their willingness, I can get up and walk.

And if I'm ever in trouble, ever crippled by fear or despair or sadness and I think I can't walk, or crawl, or breathe, it's good to know that I have friends who will carry me to Jesus.

Confessions of an Ex-Girlfriend

✦ Hi, I'm Kasey. Once, my boyfriend won me a stuffed panda at a carnival. Then he broke my heart. I dismembered the panda and left it on his front porch.

✦ Hi, I'm Jenn. When Mark and I broke up, I made copies of all of his love letters to me and mailed them to his mother.

✦ Hi, I'm Melissa. Bill and I were engaged and he called it off two months before the wedding. After everything— EVERYTHING—had been planned. I was stuck with all the deposits and reservations. The dress. Three hundred invitations. I mailed him one of our wedding invitations every single day until they were gone.

✦ Hi, I'm Angie. I work with my ex, so after we broke up, I sent myself flowers to the office and signed a guy's name.

✦ Hi, I'm Bethany, and I'm a stalker. I watched my ex for three months. I followed him on lunches and movies with friends. I drove past his house. Looked in his mailbox. I know—it's sad. I stopped.

Friends Who Carried Me

✦ Hi, I'm Kim. I wrote three songs about Matt and performed them at a coffeehouse where he and his friends hang out.

✦ Hi, I'm Jane. I didn't do anything to him. But I did eat an entire carton of ice cream every day for three months. Oh. No.

✦ Hi, I'm Lilith. After Ben and I broke up, I cut his head out of every picture I had of him. Then I burned them one by one.

CHAPTER **NINE**

Revenge: Gym Style

Non c'e amore piu' sincero di quello del cibo.
"There is no love more sincere than the love of food."

It's obvious by now that I have an issue. Okay, several issues. But who doesn't? When Ross and I broke up, my immediate reaction was: I must be too fat. Looking back, I can see that this assumption might have been a wee bit heightened by the emotional drama I was in at the time. Sorta. I might have jumped to conclusions. But hey, these are my issues to bear. So what I chose to do nine months after the breakup is really no surprise: I needed some sort of revenge. After coming to a realization that AJ's wedding was imminent and that Ross would probably see video or photographs of me as the maid of honor, I plotted my revenge.

When Ross and I broke up, all my friends and acquaintances and servers in restaurants and strangers in cars at stoplights had advice for me on how to seek my revenge. How to "get him." Like it was a game or something. One idea was to mail him a wedding invitation every day. I have three hundred invitations so that could have annoyed him

really quick. Another friend said I should send my 6'3" athlete brother up there to pound him. Someone else said I
should mail all of the wedding invitations to his friends and
family so they would think the wedding was back on and call
him to inquire. Or I should make a video of all my friends
telling him off and send it to him. All of my friends wanted
to personally call him and let him know just how unhappy
they were with his behavior. While all of these suggestions
sounded good for the moment, I chose to not do anything.
I'd like to say it's because I'm mature and above that sort of
thing, but really it's just because I was too tired and sad. I
just wanted it to fade away. Wanted to forget. AJ's wedding
relit the spark and I decided it was high time to take revenge
in the best way I knew how—by looking hot.

Don't laugh. I was quite serious. I decided to lose a few
pounds, get a nice tan, tone up, get a sexy haircut, and blow
his mind when he saw me in the wedding video. All the
folks in Boston were planning to throw AJ and Steve a party
at Christmas (in lieu of flying to California for the wedding),
and at this party would be a showing of the wedding video.
Ross would be attending the Boston gathering. And I was
going to be there too, via video. Looking hot. My goal was
for him to see me and to suddenly realize what he lost.
Smack himself in the forehead and finally get it. Tell everyone at the party that he lost the hottest woman on earth.
Every day I thought about how hot I would look. The dress.
The body. The makeup. The hair. It was a diabolical plan
absolutely perfect in it's diabolicalness. (Insert best evil vil-
lain laugh here. Mmmwaahaha.)

Now, I'm not what you would call a workout enthusiast. My idea of a good time does not involve a restrictive sports bra and sweat running in my eyes. I don't think gyms are fun. I don't want to expose my insufficiencies around other people whose insufficiencies are disguised by muscle and toning. Can't we all just jiggle and eat cake? It's not like I'm a porker. I'm quite normal, in fact. I just hate working out. I *hate* it. Hence the wrench in my perfect plan. I knew it wasn't going to be easy. I don't really have a good track record when it comes to making grand decisions to start working out.

One lazy Sunday afternoon I had big plans that involved watching a movie and eating ice cream. AJ, my health-conscious and physically fit friend, suggested I accompany her to a yoga class. *Yoga?* Unless that was a cute nickname for frozen yogurt, I wasn't interested. I was sitting. I was lounging. I was lazy. She persisted. She invited our friend Kat. Kat said, *Yoga?* She wasn't interested. She was sitting. She was lounging. Kat and I made grand speeches to AJ about how we don't need yoga to feel rested. We don't want to work out on Sunday afternoon. We're tired. We're too busy. We have very very important things to attend to immediately. We said most of these things while climbing into AJ's SUV to join her at yoga class.

As I said, I'm not what you would call a "workout" girl. I don't own "workout gear" or a snazzy sports bottle filled with liquid energy. I did buy a treadmill once, and ran on it about as many times. I exercise; I do. I just don't live and die by the early morning run. I'd rather shoot bamboo under my fingernails, actually. I don't join gyms. I don't own equipment. I don't attend Pilates classes or have a thigh master. But here I was on my way to yoga class with AJ and Kat.

We pulled into the parking lot of the local swanky YMCA in the swanky part of the swanky side of town. The front doors opened to more of a hotel lobby than a gym. Walking two steps in front of us was a fifty-year-old woman in an ankle-length mink coat. I felt underdressed. Kat and I followed AJ through a maze of hallways and short stairwells. Meanwhile, we were all three trailing after Mink Coat, exchanging puzzled smirks. Is she picking up a friend? Making a donation to the wing named after her late husband? Follow, follow, follow. Suddenly we all four rounded a corner and entered the yoga room. Kat, AJ, and I stopped short as Mink Coat removed said article to reveal her head-to-toe red leotard. *Uh-oh.* Mink Coat was the teacher.

I looked around the room to see various people in various shapes and sizes bending and twisting and centering. Most of them were wearing trendy fashionable yoga gear. I looked down and saw that I was wearing ratty old gym shorts and an eight-year-old sorority T-shirt. I felt underdressed. AJ helped us locate yoga mats and we cowered to the back of the room (not that it mattered in a room made of mirrors). I tried to "stretch" but ended up pulling a muscle before class started. *Darn.* An older gentleman entered the class wearing gray sweatpants pulled up to his armpits. I devilishly laughed—he doesn't know how to do yoga! Kat spied him as well. We were filled with cheer. Gray Sweatpants placed his mat directly in front of me. Nice. I would out-yoga this joker before he could say Downward Dog pose.

The class began. We were told to breathe in and out—
and that's about it. Kat and I felt somewhat relieved,
shouldn't there be more? Mink Coat spoke in soothing
tones that made me drowsy. Was I exercising? I mean, I've
been to classes before, but they all involved teachers who
shouted into handsfree microphones while jumping around
like their leotard was on fire. Exercise is supposed to be
loud! Mink Coat purred like a cat who's eaten an entire can
of tuna. It was far too quiet in there. Would I sweat? I felt a
bit chilly. Finally there were some instructions to raise our
arms over our heads. *Here we go,* I thought to myself. Mink
Coat lulled us through a series of "poses" that made me feel
rather silly. Kat and I kept grinning and making faces at AJ.
Everyone else in the class was earnest and serious about the
breathing and the bending; I was just trying to stay upright,
watching Gray Sweatpants like a hawk. I would not be out-
done by an old guy in an old T-shirt with old pit stains. As
he would bend, I would bend farther. Ha!

It was getting toward the end of class (I hoped) and Mink
Coat continued to sedate me with her orders. *Release the tension* seemed to be an important one; she'd been saying that
one the most. *Release the tension! Feel the earth energy!* (What? .
. . the earth what?) I was standing with my feet hip-width
apart and my head between my ankles. (Was my butt showing?) The only feeling I was feeling was the blood rushing to
my brain. I was trying to release the tension but I was too
tense about how to release it appropriately. I lifted my head
to see what Gray Sweatpants was doing just as Mink Coat
hummed at us to release the tension. Apparently Gray

Sweatpants was good at following orders. He proceeded to release his tension right . . . in . . . my . . . face.

The sound reverberated against the mirrored walls. It was so loud, I wondered if the people on the tennis courts thought a thunderstorm might be rolling in. I nearly collapsed from the—is it polite to say odor? Smell? Horrific gaseous vapor? Gray Sweatpants didn't seem fazed. Neither did anyone else for that matter. Maybe if I read *Yoga for Dummies* I would learn that "release the tension" means to let it *all* out. I looked to my left and AJ was giggling. I looked to my right and Kat was covering her mouth, holding in the heehaw. Me? I was in a cloud of green smoke.

I haven't been back to yoga class.

Clearly, exercise ain't my gig. However, revenge is. At least at the moment. And in order to achieve Operation Looking Hot, I knew that I would need to exercise and probably adhere to some sort of diet. Ewwww . . . diet. I hate that word. Almost as much as I hate the word *exercise*. In my lifetime I've successfully stuck to a diet for about fifteen minutes. That's total. I don't like diets because I like to eat. And I don't like diets because I like to eat French fries. Most diets I know about make you eat "vegetables" and cut out the fat. I'm not a huge fan of "vegetables."

I think anything fried sounds good. I think that Raisenettes are good for road trips and Reeses Pieces make any movie a better one. (Except when you think you may have dropped one in your lap but you aren't sure and it's dark and you can't find it and you're terrified that it's at that very moment melting on the backside of your jeans.) I realize that Raisenettes and Reeses Pieces are not considered diet foods, which is why I do not diet. I thought about taking diet pills for about thirty seconds. You always hear about famous people who overdose on diet pills. I've got enough tragedy, thanks. I thought about fasting, but then there's the I-love-to-eat factor. I remember in college when I would be on a date with a new Cute Boy, I wouldn't eat. I would order food that Cute Boy had paid for, and then not eat it. For some reason, I thought that the act of eating would make me appear fat and gluttonous when I was a slim size 6. I thought that if I said I wasn't hungry, I would appear thin and attractive. Again, I don't know why this insane logic made sense to me, or how I thought of it in the first place. I've grown up since then. Now, I sigh and hope Cute Boy will ask me out so I can eat and he can pay.

At the start of Operation Looking Hot the wedding was eleven weeks away. I heard about some girls in my office who were heavily into Weight Watchers. I thought about that for about three minutes and then decided I could do it. I wanted to do it. I would do it. (I think.) The appealing part of Weight Watchers for this non-dieter was that no food is off-limits. You can eat anything you want! Hooray! Sounds like the perfect plan for me! All foods have a certain point value, and you are assigned a certain amount of points per day. Easy. I signed up on-line so I wouldn't have to go to the pep rally meetings, as this would surely be a de-motivator for me, and immediately began looking up the point value of everything I like to eat. I was also looking for the loophole. The fine print. I found it. My favorite nachos?

Forty-five points. My daily point allowance? Twenty-two points. Yikes. The more I studied, the more worried I became. While it's true that no food is off-limits, one JoAnna meal would have to last me the entire week! I got hungry just thinking about it. But there was one more thing. Working out gets you *extra points*. But wait, I don't work out.

Lucky me, Sales Guy from the new gym in town ignored my office's *No Soliciting* sign and came in to talk to AJ about joining his new gym. He must have been drawn to her obvious work-out-ish-ness and talked up the new gym until we all got involved. Given my current need for food points, I went to check it out. Sales Guy met us at the door and immediately launched into his polished list of reasons to join or die. This all happened while we toured the new gym, which wasn't opening for a few more days. At the end of the tour, I found myself writing a check and nodding yes. I felt like I was in a trance. The Operation Looking Hot Trance. Sales Guy showed me the treadmills. I became excited. Sales Guy talked about Pilates classes. I drooled. Sales Guy mentioned the free tanning. I signed the dotted line.

Sounds unbelievable, I know, but I've been to the gym practically every day since. The only times I've missed have been insurmountable scheduling conflicts. When this happens I get incredibly irritated. Wait. What? I get irritated when I can't work out? I've gone completely over the edge. When the new gym had been open one week, the employees knew me by name and marveled at my dedication. If only they knew. I confessed to one trainer about

Operation Looking Hot. He encouraged me to run faster and lift heavier. That scoundrel!

It went well. I stuck to my points and worked out incessantly. I even had to go buy skinny jeans because all the ones I had no longer fit. I only had one real episode. It was one night at a surprise party for my boss, Troy. A bunch of us met over at his house and screamed *Surprise!* when he got there. His wife, Amy, informed us all that later there would be s'mores. S'mores? It became my one focus for the remainder of the evening. All the dieting and running on treadmills had left me hungry for something . . . something bad. But we weren't allowed to eat the s'mores until later because all the chocolate was in a piñata in the backyard and Troy wasn't going to hit the piñata until everyone had settled in and had some Mexican food. I went outside to stare at the piñata, hoping it would fall down and break open and I could eat all the s'mores before anyone found out. This was one week before the wedding. My willpower was waning instead of gaining. I wanted s'mores. I wanted many s'mores. I wanted them right . . . now.

All the party people seemed unaware that s'mores were on the horizon because they casually chatted and ate chips and salsa like they didn't have a care in the world. I tried to nonchalantly ask Troy when he was going to smack the piñata but he was distracted or didn't hear me. So I said it louder. It didn't help. I paced and worried, hoping no one would notice. I felt like a junkie—a chocolate marshmallow and graham cracker junkie. I was jittery and sweaty and anxious.

Finally, I managed to get everyone outside and mildly

interested. Troy found a big stick and decided to let all the kids take a whack at it. Oh great. Some three-year-old kid isn't going to be able to bust it open. All the party people thought the kids were cute and giggled at them as they each took a swing, most of them missing the chocolate, I mean the piñata, entirely. I wanted to run over and grab the stick and whack that piñata out of its misery. I had the shakes—and inside the belly of that piñata dragon was the cure. But no . . . I had to wait for all the kids to take at least four turns each. It was madness. Didn't they know I was in dire need? Didn't they know I was on the verge of insanity if I didn't get that chocolate in a timely fashion? Finally Troy whacked my chocolate free and I was able to begin assembling the s'more of my dreams.

Truth is, it wasn't as great as I thought it would be. My body wasn't used to so much chocolate and melty marshmallow. Stupid diet. I ate three s'mores anyway, just out of spite.

The week before Operation Looking Hot, uh, I mean the wedding, I polished and buffed and scrubbed and sloughed. I exfoliated and plucked and clipped and trimmed. I was ready. I had lost sixteen pounds and gotten a sexy haircut, manicure, pedicure, and my bridesmaid's dress fit beautifully. (I even had to get it taken in!) My plan was coming to fruition! I was going to Look Hot! Ross's friends, who were groomsmen in the wedding, were going to see me and flip out. They would go back to Boston and tell Ross how hot I looked. Ross would be jealous. Everything was perfect!

The day before AJ and I left for the wedding, I got sick. Of course. Of course! A runny nose and unattractive hacking cough was not part of Operation Looking Hot. I was supposed to be glamorous and classy. Untouchable, like a picture or a statue. Instead I took long naps and sniffed a lot. Great. But, when the day came I did feel pretty. I did feel that I looked better than average. At least for me.

And in all fairness, when Ross's friends saw me, they said, "Wow." And they didn't even know about Operation Looking Hot (which is amazing since I couldn't seem to keep my mouth shut about it). They were genuinely impressed with the subtle but noticeable change in me. But it didn't make me feel like I thought it would. Their reaction had been driving me for eleven weeks. Pushing me to eat healthier and run farther. To do Pilates and drink more water. I wanted them to notice—and they did. But it made me feel hollow instead of ecstatic. I didn't feel any sense of accomplishment. No victory. No just revenge.

Today I got back my pictures from the wedding and when I saw them I laughed. Because I just looked like me. I had made up some grand idea in my head that I could turn myself into someone else altogether. Someone better and braver. Someone devastatingly desirable. But I was just me with nice hair and some lip gloss. And . . . that's okay.

It's okay because I realized that I don't have to be someone else to be desirable or attractive. I only have to be me. I don't know why I wanted so much to Look Hot. I'm not sure what I was trying to prove. Maybe I wanted to feel missed. Wanted someone to be sad that I was gone—someone being Ross. I didn't want him to see me and want me back, just wanted him to realize what he lost—me. I don't know how

Operation Looking Hot became my vehicle for getting that result—and it probably didn't work anyway. I don't even know, now, if I would want it to. Because it shouldn't matter what he thinks or feels. He's no longer in my life. I think I thought it would somehow make me feel better if I knew that he was sad about that. If he wanted me back.

My friend Josephine once went through a heart-wrenching breakup, too. One rainy night she followed her ex-boyfriend while he was out with another girl. At one point she thought he saw her so she whipped her car around the first corner available and immediately slammed into a telephone pole. The damage to the car was two thousand dollars and the damage to her heart was even worse. I heard another story from a friend about a man and woman who were going through a divorce. The husband was already seeing some-one else, but was still living at home and still having his wife do his laundry. The wife wasn't happy about the divorce or the new girlfriend or the laundry. So she took all of his underwear into the attic and drug it through the insulation. He got a rash and she got revenge. But for what?

> Maybe that's why revenge doesn't really work. Because it's more about me and my erratic feelings and has little or nothing to do with him.

Maybe that's why revenge doesn't really work. Because it's more about me and my erratic feelings and has little or nothing to do with him. Ross, I'm sure, doesn't care what I look like. This whole time it's really been about me and my insecurities. My need to feel liked. The hard part about breaking up with Ross was when I realized he didn't want to be with me anymore. He was supposed to be the person who wanted me the most. Who accepted me the most. Who was proud to be seen with me and eager to spend time with me. But he ended up saying *No thanks, I'll pass*. It hurts.

Doesn't matter what his reasons were. Doesn't even matter if his reasons were entirely selfish and had nothing to do with me, the result is the same. He's there and I'm here and we aren't going to be together. I thought that if I could make him miss me, it would make me feel better. But I'm sure it wouldn't. Might even make things worse. I'm glad all I did was Look Hot. Glad I didn't mail the invitations or leave him nasty voice mails. Glad I finally realized that I'm fine with or without his approval.

CHAPTER **TEN**

Survival of the Prettiest

As a little girl I dreamed that someday I would grow up to be Miss Piggy. Every Friday night I watched *The Muppet Show*, and Miss Piggy was so glamorous. I didn't seem to notice that she was also selfish, arrogant, and bossy—and a pig. I just saw her jewelry and feather boas and I wanted to be her. That was before I knew it wouldn't be right to want to be Miss Piggy. I lived on E. 13th Street and my world was good. I was eight years old and had never really known rejection, never really felt like I didn't measure up. I knew I was smart and funny and loved. And that was enough.

One day I was riding my blue bike with the banana seat and white basket down the sidewalk when an older boy went past me on a skateboard and yelled, "Hey, Ugly!" It was the first time in my life I felt ugly or bad or wrong or unacceptable. Even though I didn't know this boy, and had never even seen him before, his words hurt. I ran back home and cried and cried to my mother—who couldn't understand why I was so upset. He was just some silly boy who made some silly comment. But it hurt me deeply.

From then on it seemed to become a constant theme in my life. I liked a boy. He liked a prettier girl. I wanted a boy to ask me to the dance. He asked a prettier girl. The pretty girls got the invitations, the boyfriends, the status. I looked in the mirror and wondered when I might become the pretty girl. If I might become the pretty girl.

My freshman year of college was the first time I felt measured against the pretty stick. I remember exactly how it felt, the first time I met the "new girl." The prettier girl. She was skinnier, perkier, and blonder and had no idea who I was. I felt like a goon looming over her, casting a shadow over her entire body. And my boyfriend was introducing me to her—and subtly letting me know that she was about to be the new me. His new lady. Of course I knew he picked her because she was prettier. I knew what their awkward giggles meant. The truth is he was young and indecisive. Or maybe he did think she was prettier. Who knows? But it was a mean start to a mean streak of being on the butt end of the survival of the prettiest.

> I liked a boy. He liked a prettier girl.

I don't know if it's always been this way, I just know that it is now. Women are judged by the exterior. Those whose exteriors match that of society's wishes are accepted. They win. If you're uber-thin and tall and your eyes aren't set too close together, then you're okay. If your thighs don't spread too wide when sitting in a movie theater seat, you will get asked out. If your butt isn't too large to sit in coach, you are acceptable.

I think for a relationship to survive, the guy has to think that the girl is really pretty right away. I've surveyed my friends, and all the successful relationships seem to start this way. When you ask the girl what first attracted her to him, she says his humor or his sensitivity or his manner. He says her hair or her eyes or her lips (or other . . . um, traits). Why is this? Is it wrong? Is it fair? Is it just the way things are? Is it the media's fault? Our own fault? Is it true that only the pretty girls deserve to get married and be happy? And what is it that defines *pretty* anyway? Who decides? (I'm not planning to answer these questions . . . just to shout them loudly and hope someone else will come up with decent answers.)

Sometimes I want to rage against the idea that beauty wins. I want to be the opposite of what everyone expects me to be. Maybe sometime I'll just get really fat and stop washing my hair. Maybe I'll let my lips get cracked and chapped and stop wearing mascara. This would surely keep romance at bay. Then I wouldn't have to deal with a broken heart anymore. Of course, my friends would still love me— except for the hair.

Singles Bible studies are always the same it seems—full of sideways glances and awkward introductions. Everyone acting as if they are there to study God's Word, not to meet someone interesting. And maybe it's both. We were told to cluster into groups of five and answer an age-old question: *What drives you?* Lots of people jumped to say money, and I agreed. Some said power. Career. Fame. After further discussion, we decided there's one main thing that drives us. Acceptance. We want money to be rich to be accepted. We want power to gain respect to gain acceptance. We want fame to be known to be accepted. We want to be prettier or thinner to be accepted. To be loved. And maybe that's the root of it all. We want to be loved.

> We want to be loved. When you have a boyfriend or a husband, strangers know that someone loves you.

When you have a boyfriend or a husband, strangers know that someone loves you. You don't have to prove to anyone that you are lovable because it's evident when you arrive at parties as part of a pair. Everyone knows. The movie ticket seller knows. The waiter knows. Your coworkers know. Someone loves you. You have been accepted. And if you don't have some visible badge of acceptance, people will simply ask, trying to find out if you're okay. How's your love life? Do you have a girlfriend? Are you dating anyone? Is there anyone special in your life? If you say no, people either feel sorry for you or look you up and down, wondering what you should fix. And it doesn't end if you are actually dating someone. Then there's, *When are you getting engaged? When's the wedding? When do you think he'll ask? Do you think she'll say yes?* I don't know about you, but these statements can tend to sound like, *Does anyone love you? Are you acceptable? Are you worth anything?*

When I was engaged it made me feel like a celebrity. Made me exciting to strangers. Made people sit up and take notice. Hey everybody, look at me! Somebody loves me! A boy thinks I'm pretty! I remember buying stationery at a card shop and the salesclerk oohhing and aahhing over my engagement ring and wanting to know all about my dress and the flowers and the cake and . . . oh yeah, the guy. If I went in today, she would tell me my total and hand me a receipt.

When you're engaged, word spreads like wildfire. I didn't complain. Fame has its advantages. Everyone, and I mean everyone, wants to know the plans. The details. The play-by-play. And I was very happy to share. It felt good to be popular—who cares the reason? Sometimes it's nice to be swept away. Sometimes it's nice to give in and wallow in the moment. Bask in the smiles and congratulations and spotlight. Some people shy away from the spotlight. Not me—I seek it out. So, being engaged was fantastic. Not only had I met the man of my dreams, not only was I in love, but the spotlight was pointed directly at me. I was aglow (probably obnoxious, too). But more than that, I was accepted. No one questioned my worthiness because I had the ring. I had the man. I was part of a pair.

It amazes me the things we will do in pursuit of acceptance. Unnecessary plastic surgery. Remain in an abusive relationship. Have a one-night stand. Starve. Lie. Drink. Spend. All the while believing that on the other side of the compromise lies a better life. Acceptance. Satisfaction. Rest. Sometimes acceptance is mistaken for rest. We run and run and seek and pursue, aiming to achieve acceptance. The idea is, once you're accepted, you can rest. All is well. Finished. If I get the job, I'll be happy. If I lose eight more pounds, I'll be happy. People will like me.

But I wonder if the other side exists. I wonder if a person can ever lie themselves into contentment. I wonder if just the right amount of plastic surgery will cure the inner ache. If starving yourself can shrink the pain. If spending more money on more clothes and more cars and more house will make you more lovable. If marrying the wrong guy just to be married will make you feel loved.

I've never seen it work. I've never seen a girl starve herself happy. I've never known someone grateful for their debt. Never heard a story of a woman enjoying the beatings by her abusive husband. Never met a girl who settled for someone less and was glad. What does the phrase *No pain, no gain* mean? I've always wondered, What's the gain part? Acceptance? Is it worth hurting ourselves? Worth the pursuit?

Then there's touch. And I'm not talking about just sex. I'm talking about good 'ol down-home regular touch. Meeting someone for the first time and shaking their hand. A friend talking to you and putting a hand on your arm. Hugs. Lately I've been dreaming that Ross and I are at the movies and he wants to kiss me or hold my hand. And every time I feel overwhelmed by his touch and wake up with a start.

I talked to a friend who had a recent shake-up. She was hanging out with some people and met a new guy. When the group moved from one location to another, New Guy took her hand and led the way. It made her feel safe. Made her feel like a princess. Special. Accepted. New Guy wasn't someone she would normally pick out of a crowd, but when he took her hand it made her think twice. It made her reevaluate and think *Maybe he's not so bad*. Behold the power of touch.

I know another girl who recently met a guy at a bar. He's not what you'd call a "catch." He's crude and disrespectful. He's crass and drunk. But he's cute, and he likes her. And he makes her feel accepted. To her, loneliness is the worst of all crimes and she is "victim of the year." Bar Guy sees her as some chick he met in a bar. She sees him as a hand to hold. A hug that feels welcoming. A place to belong and feel loved. To her, Bar Guy is the end of loneliness. An answer to the ache. The certainty that this romance will be short-lived is of no consequence. She doesn't feel lonely today. Today she feels accepted.

> I've known the power of touch. It's intoxicating.

I've known the power of touch. Taking his arm. The warmth of his embrace. His hand grazing my cheek. It's intoxicating. It makes you want more. But before long, the want becomes a need. A need we can't give up, don't want to give up. A need that can overshadow the sparseness of substance.

My girlfriends and I sometimes talk about this power of touch, even appropriate touch. I don't know how it is for other girls, but I do know how it is for me. I don't date often because I don't date casually. And when I do date someone, I expect him to draw the lines concerning the physical aspect and how far is too far (that age-old question). I expect those lines to be conservative. In fact, I'll accept nothing less. It's one of the things I loved about Ross. He respected me and he respected my body and there wasn't a question of what we would and would not do. It was an understood line, and that was so important to me.

People thought we were strange because we didn't sleep together. And by sleep together, I do not mean a euphemism for sex—I mean actually sleeping together. Like a seventh-grade sleepover without the footie pajamas. When hearing that spending the night was something we would not do, these friends would gasp and cry, *Why not?! Who will know? What's the point?* My friend Emily had a relationship in college that started out as a coworker relationship and then moved to friendship and eventually became a sexual relationship. At the time, Emily believed him to be The One. Believed that it was true love. Then he cheated on her and broke up with her, saying, *I love you . . . I'm just not in love with you.* I asked her how it was to have had sex with him—to have compromised her boundaries—and then to break up. She said the sex thing wasn't as hard to overcome as sleeping alone at night. That the hardest thing was being alone.

When did it become okay to stay overnight? When did it become okay to move in? To play house? To try things on before deciding to purchase? I don't get it. My friends say to me, *What's the big deal? We're not having sex?* All right.

Well, what are you doing? Why is it so imperative that you spend time together sleeping? If indeed there is nothing else going on, why can't you just go home? I know that I am almost alone in this stance, which is what saddens me most. Girls, my friends, are giving their hearts away too soon. Looking for acceptance in the arms of someone temporary.

I remember a time in my life when it wasn't a question. At all. It wasn't even discussed. Wasn't something my boyfriend and I needed to talk about. Maybe I was just sheltered. Naive. Now it seems that if you're a Christian and you're dating and thinking of getting married, you should live together to try things out or save money or make the transition easier. If you're not thinking of getting married, you should just stay the night because . . . it's fun, I guess? I don't know. Call me old-fashioned or conservative or closed-minded, but I think that the fear of being these exact things has led us to the edge. And it feels like I'm waving my arms furiously so that I and my friends don't fall over. I don't want to be the only one who saves marriage for marriage. I don't want to be that intimate with someone who isn't committed to me by a vow of forever. It's silly and oversaid, but true: Why buy the cow when you can get the milk for free? (No, I don't like being referred to as a "cow," but I agree with the sentiment.)

I have friends who've made some mistakes. Who felt that love conquered all and compromised for it. And usually the compromise came from believing she would be with this guy forever. From the feeling she had when she was with him. Feeling wanted and pretty and loved. That it was okay to push the boundaries a little . . . or a lot . . . because their love would last forever. And then they broke up. Seeing the hurt my friends have gone through is so painful for me. I wish I could turn back time and take away the hurt. I wish I could erase the shame. At least I can learn from them and be thankful for the decisions I've made. Of all the things that Ross did wrong, maintaining boundaries is one thing he did right. And I'm so grateful.

I learned a long time ago that I deserve someone who will wait for me. That choosing to wait is worth the occasional frustration. That acceptance isn't found in the words or arms of a man. I'm glad that of all the hurt I have gone through from breaking up with Ross, I haven't had to go through the pain of a broken sexual relationship. I don't think I'm right . . . I think that I'm trying to do what is right. What's best. Acceptance isn't found in sex. My worth isn't defined by who wants to be with me or who thinks I'm cute or sexy or fun.

My whole life, I've dreamed of it all. Being in love and hearing that someone loves me and someone wants to marry me. Meeting his family and him meeting mine. Getting engaged. Getting married. Finding the dress. Asking friends I love to be part of the event. Gazing into the eyes of the man for me. Having children together. Working it out. Growing old. It's something I've wanted my whole life. I've been skeptical of others, wondering if they were truly in love, or merely swept away. And now the finger is pointing at me. I had a glimpse. A flash. I almost made it down the aisle, but not quite. Which leaves me wondering. What happens when you get what you want, what you've been pursuing and running toward, and then it fades away? When it's robbed, stripped from you? That's what happened to me. I had it all and lost it all. I was a celebrity—now I'm a tragedy. Does that make me unlovable? Unaccepted? Did the breakup break me up?

It's not that I couldn't live without him, I just didn't want to. It's not that we can't live without someone, it's that we choose not to. What will happen if we lose the other half? If we are . . . dare I say it . . . alone? Well, I'm alone and being alone has given me time to think. And I've been thinking about what's true and what's not. Here's what I've learned so far.

It's not true that having a boyfriend meant I was acceptable. It's not true that his touch made me loved. I've tasted the drug of assumed acceptance and discovered its flaw. Looking for acceptance in a relationship can leave you brokenhearted, disillusioned. Looking for acceptance in the size of your jeans just makes you hungry.

Only Jesus. Only He can fill The Void, heal the ache, calm the storm. I think we've all said that once or twice, but is it how we live? Is it how I live? Not always . . . but I'm learning. I'm learning that the lesson I've learned thirty-two times before is still a good lesson learned. God created me to be exactly me, to show His character in a unique way. I am accepted and loved, period. Last Sunday my pastor said, *You are meant to reveal something about God that nobody else can.* That means me. That means you. It means that you're important and worthy and—accepted. Needed. Wanted. God wants you around. And no, that last sentence doesn't necessarily pacify the ache in an instant. But it's truth. And I've decided to start living in this truth, even if there are still small parts of me that need convincing. The God of all things, the God of Abraham and Moses and Paul, accepts me as I am. Wants me. Fulfills me. Likes me. And He won't abandon me, won't leave me. His love has never failed even me—you would think by now I'd get it. Psalm 136 says that His love endures forever—twenty-six times! I guess God knew I would need to hear that more than once. More than twice. More.

> You are meant to reveal something about God that nobody else can.

My pastor also says that there is no voice sweeter to God than your voice. In that case, maybe I'll talk to Him when I feel lonely sometimes. When I'm feeling defeated by the quest to be pretty enough. When I'm tempted to give in to the wrong guy just to be part of two. Instead of running from a potential hurt, maybe I'll choose to trust Him. Maybe the fact that He's never failed me once, not once, will sink in this time.

First John 3:20 says that "God is greater than our hearts, and he knows everything." Wow. Greater than my heart— the thing that controls so much of me. I don't know anyone else who is greater than my heart. If He is greater than that, the biggest part of me, I can trust Him with all that lies within. With my need for acceptance. My need to feel loved. Because I don't always understand what's going on in my heart. I don't always understand my feelings and why I react the way I do. I don't always understand why there are some things, some people, I can't seem to shake. I don't even understand the fact that God is greater than my heart. But I trust it. And I will trust—and know—that I am fully accepted in Him.

Top Ten Reasons
I'm Better Off Without Him

1. He loved his job more than me.

2. He won't go through drive-thrus.

3. He doesn't drink Diet Coke.

4. He drives only Pontiacs.

5. He likes only three bands and thinks anything by anyone other than these three bands isn't music. That's just ridiculous.

6. Driving on the interstate gives him a panic attack.

7. He will bald early.

8. He refuses to shop at supermarkets that offer "membership" or "value" cards. He thinks it's a conspiracy from the government to control his life.

9. He loves the movie *Fargo*– thinks it's "hilarious."

10. He may never love anyone more than himself.

CHAPTER **ELEVEN**

The List

It seems to me that there are some ideas imbedded so deeply in church tradition that we sometimes forget to question them. Sometimes we accept ideas as truth without really digging in and testing them to find out their worth. Sometimes things happen around us at church that we don't understand at all. But, we participate to appear as holy as the next guy. No one wants to be the outsider. The one on the prayer list with the other heathens who need to "get their lives right."

I go to Tampa every year to visit my friends Leigh Ann and Rick. One of my favorite activities on these trips is visiting Bell Shoals Baptist Church. And Bell Shoals Baptist Church is exactly the church it sounds like it would be. There are five deacons (or greeters) to shake your hand on the way in. There's a balcony for back-row Baptists and late-comers (that's us—the back-row ones, not the late ones). There's a choir loft filled to the brim with church members in choir robes belting out the latest praise and worship song. There's an orchestra pit with more choir-robed members, announcements in the bulletin, and the greet-your-neighbor time. And there's a pastor with a booming voice and funny anecdotes. It all smells like my childhood—and I love it.

Before church, Leigh Ann and Rick warned me about a certain oddity I might witness at Bell Shoals. Every Sunday, after the sermon and the invitation but before the benediction, is the offering. After the invitation amen, the pastor announces in his best wrestling-ring voice, "And now it's time for the Bell Shoals Offering!" Immediately the congregation bursts into applause and the occasional *Woo!* When my friends told me about this, I laughed and assumed the story to be a slight exaggeration. I was wrong. Just as predicted, as soon as the invitation amen was spoken, the pastor boomed, "And now it's time for the Bell Shoals offering!" People applauded. People cheered. My friends and I did the wave.

But I felt confused. Why were they cheering? Was it some inside joke that I didn't know about? I went along with it because it seemed fun enough. But I wasn't truly a participant. I asked Leigh Ann and Rick about the cheering, and they didn't know why either. It's just something they do every week.

To me, this is is just like the idea of The List. I think I began hearing about The List sometime during junior high. It must be something woven into the church's curriculum for young women. In short, The List is what you want—in a man. Your Future Husband. A Soul Mate. The List is something you're supposed to write out to God, and then wait to get it. You should write personality and character traits and if you want him to be short or tall. If you want someone funny or someone sensitive. I've even heard some suggest that you should bury your list in the yard. This makes the fulfillment of The List more successful or faster, I'm not sure which. (I also wonder if you should bury it with eye of newt under a full moon while boiling frogs legs in a black cauldron.) And I've been a part of every stage of this process. I've rolled my eyes. I've scoffed. I've written The List and waited. I've seen friends write their Lists and then get it. I've seen some write Lists and get nothing. I've even—gotten my List. (Audible gasp!)

A while ago, probably a few years by now, I was corresponding with a young man I met at a show for one of my bands. (What I mean by corresponding is that we were e-mailing and instant-messaging and talking on the phone and I was twenty-seven and he was nineteen. But I don't really want anyone to know that part.) This young man sent me one of those annoying e-mail surveys that people send around and ask you to fill out and then send back to them. These surveys always annoy me, but then I always fill them out and always forward them to all of my friends. This particular survey seemed to be tailored to his particular interest in me, though. I hadn't dated anyone in quite some time and I liked the attention, so I played along.

He didn't ask the normal questions like *Bacon bits or croutons?* or *What time is it?* or *What is your favorite fast-food restaurant?* His typical questions were *What would you like to do on a romantic date?* and *What would you want your date to wear on a romantic date?* I saw right through it, but still wanted to play along. He said nice things to me. Thought I was pretty. I might as well fill out the survey, right? One of the questions was *What would be your ideal date?* I wrote that my ideal date would be being with someone who made me laugh and made me feel special. I wrote that other than that I didn't really care. His next question was, *What would you want in your future spouse?* Without even thinking, I wrote my answer. I wrote that I want someone who gets me. Who laughs at my jokes. Someone compassionate and kind. And interesting. And funny. Someone who knows his faith isn't perfect—and that mine isn't either. Someone willing to take chances. Someone patient. Someone who knows that the exterior is fleeting and true love comes from your core. Someone who likes to watch TV with me. Someone I admire and respect. Someone who makes me feel safe.

I don't remember the response of my nineteen-year-old . . . um, friend. It didn't really matter, even at the time. I was just talking. But later I remembered this survey and e-mailed it to Ross two months after we met. I told him that he fulfilled The List. That he was every single thing I wanted. Told him that he fulfilled my dreams. And I believed he did. I knew that because he possessed every single quality I wanted, it would work between us. My mental list was more extensive than my survey answer, but Ross satisfied that too. I didn't even have to type it out and bury it in the yard. He was The List, and I was in love. Things were finally making sense for me.

People talk about making lists. They exclaim that once, long ago, they made a list of the man they wanted—all the way down to hair color and physique. Wouldn't you know it, months later this man on paper showed up and now they're blissfully, happily married! Hoorah!

156

Whenever I've heard these stories told, most people sitting around would cheer and share their own story about The List. I used to be part of this group. I used to think it sounded like a good idea and should surely work since it's worked for others. But it also made me feel like an outsider. Like being invited to the clubhouse but not knowing the secret knock. Admittance required having the Soul Mate on paper. But I did end up making a list. And then, I found him. Found my list. And we all know how the story ends. Does this mean that I made the wrong list? Does this mean God doesn't love me and wants me to go through something painful? Does this mean I deserve for my heart to be broken? Because these are suggestions I've been given. Suggestions that maybe I'm not married because I must have screwed something up. After all, isn't The List foolproof?

> So, am I to believe that God made me go through this, forced me into heartache, to teach me a lesson?

Some people who are close to me believe that God put me through this breakup to teach me a lesson or to grow me or to make me know Him more. Something like that. Like God thought it might be cool for me to meet Ross and then love him and then break up with him and cry a lot and question everything about love and life and myself and God. I disagree. If I say out loud that I disagree, their concerned faces bring up the story of Job. So, am I to believe that God made me go through this, forced me into heartache, to teach me a lesson? I'm not a scholar. I haven't attended seminary or studied ancient Greek, but I know the story of Job. And I still disagree. Because I'm not Job. I'm JoAnna. And sometimes JoAnna makes decisions after much prayer and Scripture and wise counsel. And sometimes, even then, things turn out different than expected. Sometimes that difference is painful. I don't think that anything involving unexpected pain is automatically God's decree to teach me a lesson. In fact, I think that God allows me to make decisions that He knows might hurt me, and carries me through anyway.

God's will. Two small words that seem to stir up so much controversy and doubt. Two words that can divide relationships and change the course of a person's life—not always for the best. Not because of God and His will but because of our selfish interpretation. Because of our belief that God is who we want Him to be instead of who He really is. Because of our insane need to proclaim God's will in other people's lives. God's will is something I've heard about my entire life. It was always a good breakup line in college. I went to a Baptist university full of soon-to-be preachers and soon-to-be preachers' wives. The running joke was how often guys would use the excuse of "God's will" to break up with a current girlfriend, when really they just wanted to chase the new freshmen girls. It happened to me too. A guy I was dating once (or "just talking" to) sat me down, very seriously, and explained that God had revealed to him that I wasn't the intended woman for him. He choked up, almost cried, and explained that this wasn't his decision. God had instructed him to break up with me. He was just trying to follow God's "calling" on his life. I wonder if God had also instructed him to date the new blonde on campus—because that's what he immediately did. Was this also part of God's will?

These guys were also quite good at revealing God's will for my life. Like they had an inside track or something. Unfortunately, most girls (me) would believe them and do as they were told. I once had a guy tell me that it was God's will for me to be a counselor on a youth trip he was organizing. Trick was, he had just dumped me for another girl and that girl was also going on the trip as a counselor. He tried to persuade me to go, saying it was God's will. I didn't go. (At last! A strong moment!)

When Ross and I broke up, concerned friends would ask me how I felt now, being out of God's will and all. This question puzzled me and made me feel small all at once. I had never felt so *in* God's will. In fact, I thought things couldn't have turned out any better. Yes, it hurt. Yes, I was devastated. And yet, I knew I was right where I was supposed to be. I knew that the only strength I had was coming from my heavenly Father. How could that mean I was on the outside looking in? Why would I be out of God's will just because we broke up? I suppose it's because I had gone around telling everyone that he was God's choice for me. I suppose it's because I was so sure marrying Ross was the path laid out for me. But, the fact that I didn't marry him doesn't mean things are messed up. Just because something is God's will doesn't mean that it's automatically permanent. It means that God's knowledge is bigger than mine.

Way bigger. He knew Ross and I would meet. He even knew we would break up. And He was with me every step of the way.

Others were shocked that I would let such a "godly" man go—literally shocked. Horrified. I felt as if everyone believed Ross to be the last godly man on earth and I had just ended all chances of the Christian species surviving. I heard comments like, "JoAnna, you've invested so much! This has to be God's will! Just give it time to work itself out." Huh? Sorry, but I just don't think God's sole purpose for my life is to marry. That may be part of it . . . but there's so much more that He wants for me. When my engagement ended, God's will for my life didn't end. In fact, maybe it began.

I wonder, is God's will for my life to meet only the man I marry and no one else? Seems like a pretty boring life if you ask me. I am the woman I am because of the heartbreak I've lived through. This doesn't mean I cherish heartbreak. It doesn't mean I want to go through it again. Doesn't even mean that these experiences were always God's best for me. But it also doesn't mean that they weren't. One of the things I love about God's will is that it's multifaceted. It's different for everyone. It's relationship. It's knowing Him and loving Him and allowing Him inside. On good days and bad. When you're in love and when you're not. When you find The One and when you're so lonely you can't shower without crying. God's will is for me to walk through this life with a companion. A guide. A friend. And He's all three. I was never promised Ross, but I was promised God's unconditional love. That means without condition. No strings.

Scripture tells me that He will never leave me. He will always love me. I like that. I need that.

> The closer I am to Christ, the less demanding I become about what I want.

Some might say, Well what about the desires of my heart? Psalm 37:4 says that God will give me what I desire. Right? Well, what if Ross is what I desired? Why didn't I get what I desired? I think there may be more to this verse than we want to realize. The NIV reads, "Delight yourself in the LORD and he will give you the desires of your heart." I've heard people interpret this verse as a "gimme" for everything they want. I desire a new car. God says He will give it to me! I desire more money. God says He will give it to me! I desire a husband. A healthy baby. God is a provider and a generous giver—but not a vending machine.

My pastor, Pete, once placed a vending machine onstage during his sermon to represent the way we treat God sometimes. We say, *I want a better job!* We hit the Better Job button on the vending machine and wait impatiently for one to fall down into the tray. We read Psalm 37:4 and think it's the magic key to the treasure box full of all God's blessings. This, to me, is The List. It kinda feels like I'm limiting what God can do in my life. Kinda feels like I know what I need and I'm telling Him to give it—now! But I know that I don't know what I need.

My friend Mark told me that The List for him was a tall

girl with dark hair. He married a short girl with red hair. And even though his wife may be opposite from what he thought he wanted, she's the only girl for him. God's best. And Mark could have missed her if he had held out for The List Girl, who may or may not exist. The first part of Psalm 37:4 says to delight ourselves in the Lord. I've learned (the hard way) what this means. The closer I am to Christ, the less demanding I become about what I want. The more I know Him, the more I can see and understand what His best is for me. Sure, I still mess up sometimes. I still find myself pressing buttons on the vending machine and waiting for my wants to appear. I still tap my foot impatiently when things don't go my way. But, I also find that when I truly seek Him, when I truly delight myself *in Him* . . . my wants become smaller and He becomes greater.

So, I found my List and then lost him. Am I a loser? Does this mean that I messed up? No. It means that no man, no list, will ever complete me. No man can satisfy. That only in Jesus can I find a hope that doesn't disappoint. It's not about lists or mates or being married or single. It's not about who has a man and who doesn't. It's not about who thinks you're pretty and who doesn't. It's about the love of a Savior that is unconditional. It's about finding contentment in the One whose love endures forever.

CHAPTER **TWELVE**

Don't Underestimate the Power of Matches:
You Might Get Burned

I have some friends who have been utilizing the latest dating craze—on-line dating. Don't worry, this isn't a commercial for on-line dating. At least, I don't think it is. Seems like in the past few weeks I've heard one too many stories of friends of mine admitting to meeting people on-line . . . and liking it. Even meeting people in person! From a Web site? I've also seen some of the more popular sites surreptitiously advertised on various conservative Christian Web sites, and (gasp!) I even saw a commercial for one on network TV! The commercial aired during a tear-jerking reshowing of a favorite chick flick, *Hope Floats*. What?! Do the stodgy executive suits think that a bunch of single women will be sitting around on a Sunday night watching *Hope Floats* on TV? My single girlfriends and I were appalled. The indignation! The nerve! These slick advertisers think they have us all figured out, do they? They think we're desperate just because we're drooling over Harry Connick Jr.? They think we have nothing better to do than surf the Web for our very own hunk of burnin' love? So I went onto one of the biggest sites just to see what all the fuss was about.

I will say this. For on-line meat markets, these Web clubs certainly do a good job selling themselves. After being on one site for all of thirty seconds, I too began to believe that my Soul Mate just might be there waiting for me. My match. That's the term they use—*match*. Like I'm a three-legged chair in search of some stability. I began to believe that I must fill out, must join, must match!

I quickly exited the site before it was too late. But alas, it was too late. Upon exiting, a pop-up jumped onto the screen and asked me why in the world I exited without signing up? Even though it was merely a typed message in a pop-up window, I felt guilty. Like I had abandoned a friend stuck talking to the weirdest guy at the party. The question was almost whiny. "Whyyy did you leeeeave? You didn't even say good-byeeee." Various reasons for leaving were listed, and I was instructed to check the appropriate box. I wrote my answer in "Other," stating that "Since I have recently broken up with my fiancé and that situation has left a huge gaping hole in my heart, I believe I have no need for love or boys or matching or soul-mating thankyou-verymuch." The blank was too short so my answer read, "Since I have recently."

Again, I hit the X to escape my peril when yet another exasperating message appeared. This new message told me that since I obviously wasn't emotionally or intellectually prepared to meet the absolute love of my life, then when I returned to the site, as I most assuredly would, they guessed I could have a FREE Month's Membership (with purchase of one month for $49.99), you sad loser. (Really it just said we'll give you a free month should you choose to return, but I could read between the lines.)

I thought about that for a while. On just about every page of the site was an ad to get a FREE personality profile that would shed light on my relationship tendencies. Allegedly, no strings attached. It's always a good thing to learn about yourself, right? Always good to grow and mature. Apparently this site had a short five-hundred-question survey that would reveal all things relational and help me discover my one true love. And I do love a challenge. So I decided to take the test.

I've taken personality tests before. Most of the questions I could fly right through because I've answered them on more than one occasion. Do you enjoy reptiles as pets? No. Do you like to read? Uh-huh. Are you funny? Very. Would your friends classify you as dull or a bore? Never. Man, these five hundred questions were going to be a piece of cake. (Mmm . . . cake.) But I wasn't prepared for what lay ahead.

I think I'm pretty good at knowing myself. I've known myself my whole life, in fact. I know what I like and what I don't like. I know how I will react in certain situations and how I hope other people will react in those certain situations. I'm extroverted except when I'm introverted and I'm outgoing until I'm shy. The one hang-up I have seems to plague every woman I know—I don't know what I really look like. Sure, I've seen myself in the mirror. Lots of times. But if I drew a picture of myself, it would be radically different from what my friends might draw. And mine might be better or it might be worse—depends on the day, I mean moment.

> Women have blinders when it comes to seeing them-
> selves accurately.

Women have blinders when it comes to seeing themselves accurately. At least the women I know. And I don't mean the need to build up self-confidence or praise the spirit of woman or anything like that. I mean honest to goodness knowing what you look like. Most women tend to exaggerate the negative and completely forget the positive. There are the chosen few who feel that God's earth was made for them to walk upon and their presence makes creation complete, but I'm not talking about those girls. I'm talking about me and my friends and how we always think we're too fat or too short or too pale or too plain or too hippy or too hairy or too . . . not who we think we should be. I think I'm fairly accurate when it comes to understanding the way my friends look. Just not myself. Which brings us to the horrible rotten no-good section of the meet-your-mate questionnaire.

Five words were listed and I had to rate myself from "Not at all" to "Very much" for each word. The first word was *Beautiful.* I waited so long to answer that the survey timed out and I had to log in all over again (to my relief, it kept the 480 questions I had already answered). I looked for the "No, but I used to be" option, but it wasn't there. So I waited. I'm not sure what I was waiting for, I just waited. And I got timed out again. There was no space to write in my answer of "Not exactly but I think beauty comes from the inside" or "I'm better than some and worse than some" or "Who do you think you are to ask me such a question, you shallow pig?" *Glamorous?* Yes. *Beautiful?* Uhhh . . . I tried to focus on the second word and come back to *Beautiful* but the second word was worse—*Sexy.* Again, I wanted to write in my answer of "Depends on who you ask 'cause the waiters at Las Palmas give me the Foxy Discount" or "I find this question degrading and therefore refuse to answer" or "Do you have a space for very much plus?" I moved on to the third word and it didn't get any better—*Fit.* Should I mention that I'm doing Weight Watchers and I've been running and doing Pilates and I've lost sixteen pounds? Is there really a universal definition of what makes a person fit? Or sexy? Or beautiful?

I struggled through this portion of the questionnaire and finally finished. I was promised a detailed report of my relational profile—as well as some sample "matches" that I could converse with if I chose to sign up. (Read: Pay money.) Three days later I received four matches who were absolutely fashioned by God to fit with me—at least by the site's standards and preferences. I read about each guy but saw no photos (no pictures can be seen unless you sign up and pay your fee) and laughed. Two live in Kentucky and two live right here in Nashville. One of them I'm pretty sure I used to hang out with, and I *know* he's not my Soul Mate. One of them sounded gay, so I'm pretty sure I'm not his type. The two in Kentucky sounded interesting. But I laughed because it made me think about how I met Ross. We e-mailed. We called. We discovered all the things about us that "matched." We met through friends instead of a Web site, but it's all the same. We had so many things in common that there was a brief scare that we might be the same person. By all standards—psychological and relational and spiritual and physical and emotional—we were a *match*. I believed it. He believed it. Our families believed it. Most of our friends believed it. And then we broke up. So, why should I pay $49.99 a month to discover that someone else who likes the same movies as I do and has the same background as I have isn't necessarily the one for me? I'm not sure. I just chalked it up to research and called it a night.

That's the bad part about these on-line dating services. If a girl "meets" a guy by reading his criteria—which is essentially a step above his putting his best foot forward—she will instantly know he's The One. She'll think about how they'll meet and how they'll fall in love and how he will propose (and oh! he'll do exactly what she has always dreamed of) and where they will live. You know this is true. Girls can fantasize an entire lifetime off one dreamy comment. Like if he says his grandmother was the most influential person in his life, you automatically assume he's ultra-sensitive to women's needs and will never let you down, ever. In reality, he probably wrote that his grandmother was the most influential person in his life so you would think he's ultra-sensitive to women's needs and go on a date with him.

Don't Underestimate the Power of Matches

Girls (including me) have an insane ability to create some-thing from nothing. To talk for four hours straight about a glance, a sigh, a wink that could have just been dirt in his eye. Don't get me wrong. This is not male-bashing. I'm simply pointing out that to dream—and dream in this case means to conjure up a false reality—can only lead to disaster. Some women take years to get over a breakup with a man they never dated. Take me for example. I fell in love with my best friend. Remember Jack? He was exciting. He made me feel like somebody. I had never really felt like a nobody, but he made me feel like someone deserving. He told me I was dif-ferent from all the other girls he had gone out with. He said there was just something about me. I wanted to be with him. All the time. I think I even wanted to *be* him. And I think I knew that he wasn't my boyfriend. (Didn't I?) But I also knew that he loved me more than anyone else ever had. He told me I was special and hilarious and smart and real. He loved that I was real. Apparently all the other girls around were big phonies and I was the only real thing going. At least, that's what he told me. And I believed him.

> Girls (including me) have an insane ability to create something from nothing.

I remember him once calling me at work in the middle of the day. This was after we had both graduated from col-lege and were living six hours apart. He was in seminary and I was working retail. His call startled me and I thought

169

something must be wrong for him to be calling long-distance in the middle of the day while I was at work. He said no, he just wanted to hear the sound of my voice. That's right, he just wanted to hear the sound of my voice. When he said it I felt like everything around me blurred and swirling background music began to play. That had to count for something. And it did. With me at least. I thought his words had meaning and depth and qualified us to be together forever. But he just thought I was a cool girl who was fun. And that was it.

However, this wasn't my first experience with fictitious romance. There was also my Far Side Buddy from high school. Every morning of my senior year there would be a new Far Side cartoon taped to the top shelf of my locker with a note from him. My crush. We sat next to each other in English. We walked to class together. I practiced writing my first name with his last name. We spent my entire senior year together. We were both planning to attend the same college the next year. Oh yeah, and he had a girlfriend. But I knew . . . *knew* . . . that it was me he loved. We did end up going to college together. He's now happily married to the girl he dated the year he was my Far Side Buddy.

It seems as if the hardest breakups in my life have been the fake variety. When I would build an entire relationship, an entire future, in my mind. This boy and I would be a perfect match. All my friends agreed that the signs were obvious, all pointing to yes. When things didn't go as I had hoped and dreamed, I would be shattered. I've also experienced the opposite effect. I'd have a crush on a guy from afar, dreamed up an entire life for us together, and when we finally did go out or hang out, I was disappointed. He wasn't what he was supposed to be! He wasn't what I'd made him to be. There was one guy in college that I'd exchanged flirty glances with in the cafeteria. I knew very little about him but felt free to dream up the rest. I knew he would eventually ask me out and our first date would be a dream come true. He did eventually ask me out. And he did turn out to be nothing that I thought he was. In fact, he turned out to be a thug. It's pathetic, I know. The only reason I'm telling on myself is because I have tons of friends who have done the same thing. What makes us slip from reality to fantasy so easily? How do the lines get blurred to the point of no return?

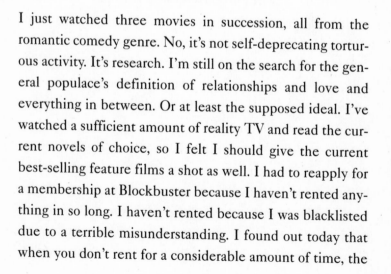

I just watched three movies in succession, all from the romantic comedy genre. No, it's not self-deprecating torturous activity. It's research. I'm still on the search for the general populace's definition of relationships and love and everything in between. Or at least the supposed ideal. I've watched a sufficient amount of reality TV and read the current novels of choice, so I felt I should give the current best-selling feature films a shot as well. I had to reapply for a membership at Blockbuster because I haven't rented anything in so long. I haven't rented because I was blacklisted due to a terrible misunderstanding. I found out today that when you don't rent for a considerable amount of time, the bulging computer system kicks you out, so, after happily obliging to the obligatory application, I am a happy member once again. To the shelves!

I picked out the three movies with the most copies on the shelf. The ones everyone has seen and rented and bought. The ones that I'm supposed to mimic. The ones that should make me sigh and dream goofy dreams with a goofy grin on my face. After all, in the end doesn't the guy always get the girl? I know this even before taking the movies home to watch. Romantic comedies are not meant to be about mystery and intrigue. They really aren't about heartache either. Sure, there might be a splash of heartache thrown into the beginning, but it's never going to be the end result. The end result will always be about the guy getting the girl . . . it just might be told in a different setting with a different girl. And isn't that what we ultimately want? To be the girl who ends up with the hero? The flashy smile? The charmer? We want to be swept away with swelling background music to speed us on our way.

I watched the movies and didn't learn anything new. The message to me is the same: Be beautiful and helpless and a man will come and save you. The end. But I've been living my life for a while now and it doesn't seem to go that way for me. It doesn't even really happen on "reality" shows that aren't supposed to be scripted. Shortly after Ross and I broke up, I hung out with a group of girlfriends to watch the finale of *The Bachelorette*. We laughed as the final two contestants vying for the Bachelorette's heart were sized up by family and friends, and we sighed as speeches of undying love were professed. We screamed in delight when she picked the least likely guy and pretended to not care when he got down on one knee and asked her to be his wife. I laughed and talked and screamed along with my friends— but inwardly I retreated. The story line hit too close to home. My broken home. The reality of this reality show is that these two lovers who are now betrothed have known each other for six weeks. And in that six weeks have spent only a few days together—all under the spying eyes of cameras and producers and millions of American eavesdroppers. They have wined and dined in the finest of restaurants, worn upscale-retail sponsored clothes, lived in Malibu luxury and . . . six weeks and hundreds of commercials later, they are in forever love.

In her long-awaited speech, the bachelorette told the man she chose, "This day is a day I dreamed about my entire life. I see smiles and laughter. I see babies and grandbabies. I see comfort and safety. I see me in a white dress and I see it with you." The lucky guy replied that he loved her back "with every ounce of who I am." Don't misinterpret and think I'm making fun—I was on the edge of my seat along with the rest of the viewing public. I, too, hope that their love will last for all eternity, or at least longer than the other reality relationships that haven't even outlasted the reruns. But it made me think.

I have a white dress. I have the perfect white dress and the perfect veil. It's my aunt Beverlee's veil that my grandmother hand made twenty-seven years ago. It's exquisite and breathtaking. I was supposed to be wearing that perfect white dress and that perfect veil twenty-three days from the finale of *The Bachelorette*. I was going to walk down the aisle to the perfect song on the perfect day surrounded by perfect flowers and perfect candles—and marry the perfect guy. I had never been so sure of anything in my life. My fairy tale was coming true. The day I had thought about my entire life. It was really happening. Everything I had ever wished for, he was. Everything I had longed to hear, he said. I had finally found The One. My match. I lived in Boston a total of seven days. Seven days. How can a love that was supposed to last a lifetime unravel in seven days?

The white dress is still hanging in the closet. The flowers and candles were canceled. The musicians were told not to come. And I'm expected to survive and keep living and go on without. I guess I should be glad that all of America isn't concerned about how the relationship is going. And it's left me wondering what it truly means to love someone. I watched the TV couple profess undying love—not *attraction* or *like* or *you're-kinda-cool*. They promised to *love* each other forever. Do they really know what love means? Do they really understand? Do I? I thought I did. I thought I had found what my heart had always longed for. Thought I had found forever. But in reality—the real reality without cameras and producers and editing—I didn't. That is the reality that I must face every day.

I get nervous that I made it up. That he loved me only in my head. That I had done it again. That I had convinced myself he was my Soul Mate when really he was just some guy. It's like the dangling carrot, this elusive Soul Mate. At least to me. People talk about it as if it's a course you should take in college or a learn-at-home tutorial. A rite of passage. Finding The One. I'd like to know the rules, since I seem to be so bad at it. Can there be more than one? Is it possible to meet a Soul Mate, it doesn't work out, and you meet another one? Is a Soul Mate only the person you marry? And if that's true—what is a Soul Mate? I wouldn't know, never having found one. I thought I did. Twice. What's wrong with me that I could get such a huge thing wrong—twice? Ugh. Just the thought of it makes me queasy. Girls in the movies can meet and "just know" someone is their Soul Mate in a span of two hours on screen. I can't seem to do it in my lifetime.

It's amazing how different you can be from someone you share so much with. Amazing how you can think so exactly the same on so many levels and yet be miles apart. Years apart. A lifetime apart. But the likenesses are easier to see up front—a lot like buying a house. When house hunting, you walk into the vast and airy foyer, which may later become a dingy entryway with stained carpet. You marvel at the vaulted ceilings and crown molding, which just takes your eyes off the crack in the floor that hints at a crack in the foundation.

That's me. I move a lot, so I've at least walked through most of Nashville's apartment selection. My biggest concerns when walking through the empty models are the closet space and cabinet space. Where can I put my stuff? I don't think about the foundational issues or plumbing issues; that's the apartment complex management's problem should anything arise. My friends John and Nivah are in the throes of selling their house and hopfeully buying a new one. Everyone involved in this buying-and-selling process is quite concerned with the foundation. The roof. The structure. The hidden problems that aren't as easy to see. Not me. I ooohh and aaahh at the shiny stuff. The cool refrigerator or the spacious bonus room—the extras. The fancy doorways and spiraling staircase. If the foundation is rotting I wouldn't know it. I feel secure because the closet is enormous.

I wonder if that's what happened with Ross and me. I wonder if the foundation was cracked from the start. At the time, I didn't think it was. I even talked with Ross about how secure and sound we were. Answered questions from my parents and his parents and our friends, saying, *Yup, Safe and secure.* Solid. Something we can build a life on—our life, together. But I'm not sure if I looked, really looked. Meaning, going in the scary cellar with a flashlight. Checking the crawlspace that's dark and has bugs and creepy crawly things. That uncomfortable place. It's not a fun place to go, but it's really the only way to get a good look at the infrastructure. Did I look there? I wonder if I was distracted by fancy fixtures and a great laugh.

I did end up signing up and taking that Web site's free-month offer. I've talked to several guys who are supposed to be perfectly matched to me. I don't get it. Or maybe I don't trust it. One guy asked me to "honestly" tell him what my intentions were, because he wanted to meet me in person. So I told him "honestly" that I signed up only to see what it was all about, and to do research for my book. He hasn't written me back.

CHAPTER **THIRTEEN**
Knowing

The low-fuel light on my dashboard keeps flickering on and off, taunting me. Pointing and laughing at me. I can hear it singing *I might die, I might die, you'll run out of gas and I'll just die.* The low-fuel light and the empty gas tank are staging a coup, and I'm the enemy. My friend Nivah has warned me of the dangers of running out of gas. She's sort of an unauthorized expert since she's run out at least twice. But not me—I'm an escape artist. I can drive forever because I have a Honda. Everyone says Hondas last forever and I'm putting that to the test. I've never run out of gas. Therefore, I have some innate resistance to fueling up when it's time. I always think I have more time. More miles. More starts and stops. I can't be bothered to get gas; I don't have time. I'm too busy. Putting gas in my car is a nuisance that I like to avoid.

Car maintenance. Yuck. It's my least favorite thing to do. I abhor it. Within this category is getting gas, oil changes, a tag renewal *every* year, fixing what is broken, rattling, or smoking and general cleaning. All of these things I hate. I just want to get in, turn the key, and reach my desired destination with no trouble. Is that so much to ask? It seems endless. There's always something to clean or renew or replace.

I don't mind other upkeeps as much. I clean the kitchen and my closet. I wash the sheets on my bed once a week, and that takes way more effort than putting gas in my car. I can't explain it. I just hate it. I'm jealous of Fred Flinstone. His car didn't have a timing belt or a gas tank. Just feet. I want a Fred Flinstone car so that I don't have to worry about anything. I can just do it myself. Oh, wait. That last sentence was a bit too revealing.

It's everywhere lately. In every magazine and catalog—DIY. Apparently, it's the new hip way to purchase. The first time I saw this phrase I didn't get it. DIY? But I quickly figured it out and understood the appeal. The allure. Ohhh . . . Do It Yourself. Of course. You can get a DIY bookshelf or a DIY ceiling fan. There's probably even a DIY kit to learn car maintenance. DIY plumbing. DIY cabinet installation. Home Depot is an entire store dedicated to doing it yourself. (And it works. When I walk through there, I feel like I can build or fix anything!) More and more, society is telling me that I don't need anyone. Just me. I can do it myself. I can build furniture and make a dress and unclog the sink, put up miniblinds and get over him . . . all by myself.

I once heard a Christian evangelist preach about filling up my love tank. I rolled my eyes and giggled. Love tank? It was the lamest thing I had ever heard. He went on and on about all the different ways to fill up your love tank and care for your love tank. I don't remember most of what he said, but I remember the basic idea. People need Christ.

People need people. And people need love. (Cue The Beatles, "All You Need Is Love.") I'm reminded of this concept—The Love Tank Concept—as my low-fuel light continues to flicker. And I realize that there may be more to this silly tank business than I originally thought.

Lately I've been run down. Tired. I get up tired and I go to bed tired. And yawn throughout the day. I'm tired because I'm busy. Busy working and busy writing. Busy teaching and busy planning and busy getting on with my life. There's barely enough time to shower. I've been so busy trying to put myself back together that I haven't had time to think about fueling up. I think my tank may be empty. A lot of the time, I feel blank. Ready to quit. I can see the warning light blinking in my head, but I'm still trying to squeeze out ten more minutes on the treadmill. Ten more hours of work. Ten more words on paper. There are so many records to sell and so much blank paper to fill, I cannot rest. This is all fine and good. Some might even classify it as a healthy drive, but I call it running on empty. And I'm feeling it most in my heart. I've been so busy running around pursuing the DIY that I've almost given out.

I also notice that relationships are the first thing to go in my life when I'm running on empty. I edge everyone out to make more room for the things I do for them. I edge out the things I hold most dear. People. And, more important, Christ. The One who accepts me as I am. Who loves me completely. Who knows that sometimes I miss Ross and sometimes I'm still sad. Who knows that sometimes I feel like no man will ever love me again. Who knows all the parts of me, good and bad. Even the dark parts that make me run until I'm empty. I stop talking to Him because I'm tired. Stop reading His Word because I'm tired. It's ridiculous. Writing it down is shameful. Maybe I'm consumed with DIY. Maybe I think the more activities I participate in, the less likely I am to be lonely. Maybe I think I can do it myself—that I am my own island. But being my own island has left me depleted. Vacant. I need a refill. I need to soak Him in. I need to dive into His love and float for a while.

I wonder why I make it so difficult. I wonder why I run and run until I'm all used up. Shouldn't I share myself with Christ when I'm full? Shouldn't I give Him the best parts of me instead of the empty residue? I think it's about a daily refill. A daily drink. A daily choice. I can choose to meet Him every day, or I can choose to push my limits and run on empty. There's risk involved. I could lose power at any moment. Without my energy source, I can't perform at my best. I'll be slower and break down faster. Either way, it's up to me to stop and fill up or to run on empty. I need to fill up so that I can face those things in my life that slow me down and hold me down. Like my fears. Specifically, the fear that I will be alone.

> I've always had a Cinderella view of love.

I've always had a Cinderella view of love. I always suspected that when I met The One it would be rapture and fireworks and unarguable concrete confidence. I knew that

I would just *know*. That's what we're told, right? At singles conferences and Bible studies and in books for the lonely and by friends who've found it. You just *know*. Oh yeah, and you should never ever settle for anything less than *knowing*. Sounds easy. Sounds like you could just bump into someone at Target or at an intersection and you would just *know*. Well, I shop at Target and I've had a few run-ins at intersections and I don't really *know* anything. In fact, I've always wondered what it is exactly that I'm supposed to *know*. All the advice from my past has failed to mention what it is that you *know*. You just simply *know* . . . at least that's what I'm told. This foretelling advice is usually accompanied by some cheerful wink or nudge, which causes me to roll my eyes and change the subject. It's like you're not in the club until you *know* and until you know what this *knowing* actually is, you're doomed to be winked at and whispered about. There's allegedly no way to look for or figure out the *knowing*. Once again, you just *know*.

Sometimes I look around and gasp. How can women—beautiful and talented and interesting and hilarious women—fall into the arms of such unsuitable men? I see it all the time. I see women in restaurants being verbally abused by men they choose to be with, women in the mall being belittled at a store counter, women being yelled at in cars at a stoplight. I see my friends settling for someone less than exciting. I hear them exclaim, *I just knew!* and then see the disappointment in their eyes when they discover they didn't *know* after all.

I see it in women I know and women I hear about. It's a constant sitcom theme and movie-of-the-week drama.

Women who seem drawn to, well, anyone. Women who just want to have someone. It's almost as if the status of having someone—anyone—is better than being alone and fine. As if the embrace of the wrong man is better than no embrace at all. Have we come to accept this as truth? Do we suddenly find it suitable to spend our lives with "okay" and "not spectacular" just so that we can be part of two? Is being in an "okay" relationship truly better than being alone? Is the stigma of being yourself by yourself too horrible to endure? Is the embrace of any man worth giving ouselves away? No. I refuse to accept this. I don't want to be with just anyone. I want to be with someone who is passionate about Jesus and hilarious and fun and smart and interesting and giving and kind and . . . I just want the best. The best! I won't settle for anything less.

Oops. I settled.

At least that's how it's starting to feel. Me, the tireless preacher of not settling. I was driving home from work, thinking about Ross, who is now just another notch on the what-once-was tally, trying to make myself miss him. (Not sure why—I love the drama?) That's when I realized the ugly truth. The only part about him that I miss now is the physical. I miss his touch. I miss his lips. I miss his embrace. The way he looked at me that made me feel pretty. That spark disguised as *knowing*. And that's it. I don't miss anything else.

Upon realizing this, I felt ashamed. Embarrassed, even. I immediately warned myself not to divulge this dirty little secret to anyone on earth, as it would blow my cover of being the tireless preacher of not settling. Then I promptly went home and told my roommate, sighing that I've become that very thing I protest. I settled—for the embrace. For the kiss. For the comfort and assumed place to belong. Settled for someone instead of The One. After proclaiming to the world that finally I just *knew*, I realized that I didn't. Could this be true? I don't think, in actuality, it's the entire truth. There was so much more. There were lifelong wishes that seemed to come true with him. There were things I never knew I wanted that he was. He answered all the longings and satisfied all the needs. But who he has now revealed himself to actually be is nothing of the man I loved. His facade faded and the reality of him was devastating. Therefore, the only thing I miss is the one thing I no longer have. The touch. The kiss. The embrace.

> I finally understand what it means to be complete in my identity in Christ.

Because . . .

Because I have every other thing. Before I met him, my life was fulfilled. I had a relationship with the Savior of my soul, authentic friendships, a place to use my God-given talents, a good-better-best job, true family . . . the list goes indefinitely on. These things, the things that matter and make up the woman that is me, have not gone. My relationship has gone. My status of being part of a couple has gone. The kisses have gone. But I remain. And this makes me happy. Happy because I think I've finally grown up, while continuing to grow. I finally understand what it means to be complete in my identity in Christ. What it means to not need another person to define who I am. Having a boyfriend did not define me. Having a fiancé did not define me. Therefore, losing a fiancé did not ruin me. All the parts of me that are good have survived.

I still feel the stigma. It's still difficult to arrive at a party of couples and be the only "single." I still miss the embrace. But I'm satisfied in knowing that the embrace doesn't make me . . . and the lack of it didn't break me. I know that I am lovable and worthy. I know that I have a Savior who accepts me as I am and provides my every need. I know that no man—no man—can be all that I need. No man can make me feel truly accepted. Only in Christ can I be beautiful and complete.

I do hope to one day again meet a man whose arms are familiar and whose smile warms me. But, I don't view today as a waiting period to get into the *knowing* club. Today is a day to find joy in my Creator, the Lover of me! Today is a day to be the woman Jesus sees, the woman He loves. And that is something I am sure of. That is something . . . I just *know*.

EPILOGUE

Flirting Again

It's the worst feeling when your heart and your head disagree. When the argument between them makes you feel like you might burst right in two. When your head says you're fine and your heart says run for cover. When concerned friends ask what's wrong and you have no answer because you don't really know. That's me today. On the verge of tears and nothing to be sad about. I have an uncontrollable frown. And I woke up with this feeling and no explanation. It's true that the last few nights have been riddled with nightmares, but that's not so unusual. So where did this mood come from? This cloud? I got to work and studied my calendar of things to accomplish, noticing the date. The knot in my stomach lurched. March 15. Aha.

It wasn't so long ago that March 15 had the opposite effect on my emotions. Ross and I chose it as our wedding day. It should be the happiest day. The best day. Some said I should beware the Ides of March (complete with a ghoulish tone and scary face) and I giggled. Ides? Who cares? All I knew was that I was getting married to the man of my dreams on March 15—my new favorite day. And it couldn't come soon enough.

Today's feelings are a bit different. Opposite. Today feels heavy and tragic. But instead of being sad it just makes me angry. It's been a year! I'm over him! I don't miss him! I don't want to relive the past or get it back or try again. I'm glad I'm here and not there. I'm glad to be on the other side of the heartbreak. The good side. Today should be a day of mass celebration! Heartfelt jubilation! Joy in the present, which is brimming over with good things! Huge great things!

And I'm tired of talking about the past. I'm tired of writing about it and thinking about it and rehashing it over and over. People are tired of reading it. Enough already. It's high time I started writing about something else. Anything else. Time this canceled-wedding nonsense was over. I'm annoyed. I want to shake my heart by the shoulders and tell it to straighten up. Act right. Move on.

The harshest reality I've ever experienced (after learning that Santa Claus supposedly isn't real) was when the man I loved became a stranger overnight. Someone I didn't recognize. I was suddenly standing next to an unknown. A puzzle. A mystery. I felt connected and disconnected all at once. Like I should introduce myself to this person who looked a lot like someone I used to know. Used to understand and love. I wanted to stay with him forever and I wanted to run as fast as I could. Outrun the heartache. Outrun the end of us. Out with the new and in with the old. In with the old memories and feelings and expressions. First kisses and secret glances. The old feelings of belonging and everything making sense. The newness of confusion and doubt and separation was too much. I wanted to go back.

I like being single. For real. I do. I like making my own schedule and watching whatever I want on TV and eating cereal for dinner. I like sleeping late on Saturdays. I like deciding to go to a movie on a weeknight fifteen minutes before it starts. I like spending wild amounts of money on my friends. I like going out of town at the drop of a hat. All these things sound selfish and maybe they are, but being single is fun and spontaneous and unscheduled and great. Free. But today I felt bound by my state. Chained to my singleness. Destined to wander the earth by myself, wailing about what once was. The modern Miss Havisham. At least I haven't been wearing my wedding dress for the past year.

And to make matters more interesting, I'm dating again. Sorta.

It's bizarre. When Ross and I broke up, it was like my Flirt-Finder ran out of batteries. Pre-Ross, I would have been able to tell you how many cute boys were in a five mile radius. Post-Ross, Cute Boy could come and sit right next to me and I wouldn't know it. Actually, that's what happened recently. A cute boy came and sat right beside me, and I didn't even notice him.

So now I'm back in the dating game, which tends to get expensive. I find myself shopping the makeup aisles of every discount and department store, looking for anything that will make me cuter and flirtier and more presentable.

And I'm a sucker for packaging. I think the cosmetics industry knows this because they rush to my aid by printing what I need to know right on the packaging. This will make you glamorous. This will make your lips sexy. This will make your hair shine and boys will like you. This blush will make you look shy and approachable. The shade of blush I wear is called "Glamorous." Go figure.

The other night I was in Wal-Mart, thinking about my crush, and I once again found myself in the makeup section. Sometimes I feel like Bonne Bell has implanted a chip in my brain that shouts into my subconscious "You must be pretty. Makeup makes you pretty. Buy more makeup." I zone out and follow the voices in my head. I must, because there's really no other way I could have ended up buying so much, well, I don't really want to say. It's too embarrassing.

I'm twenty-nine years old, but I think Lipsmackers still rule. Sure, I wear grown-up lipstick sometimes, but nothing beats Bubble Gum Lipsmackers. Every girl has her favorite. Dr. Pepper. Watermelon. The old standbys. I was shopping the Bonne Bell section when somehow I drifted a little to the right and found a world of interesting new colors and fun packaging and shiny cases. Guys say that their eyes glaze over in the electronics section. For me, it's the lip gloss aisle. I was innocently enough looking for something new and fun from Lipsmackers when I stumbled across this sea of silver boxes and glittery cases and eye shadow colors that gave me the shivers. I shouted to my roommate Jen to hurry over, that I had found the mother lode. She grabbed and I ransacked until we both had two fistfuls, and that's when we saw it. The perky sign and picture at the top of the display—Mary Kate and Ashley Olsen. I screamed and ran. I am twenty . . . nine . . . years . . . old. I cannot, I repeat cannot, wear Mary Kate and Ashley Olsen makeup!

It's not my fault. The only reason I was even in that aisle is because I wanted something new to look cute for someone new. Then I realized, why bother? I've been out with or talked to several guys in the last few months. Guys with potential and great résumés and even some with great hair. One guy called me and gushed about how "cool" I am and how much he "enjoyed talking to me" and how he couldn't wait to "talk" to me again. Then he never called back. I went out with another guy who couldn't stay off his cell phone long enough to say hello to me. Another guy, Hot Guy, surprised me one day by showing up at my office and hugging me. He has the kind of arms you don't know about until he puts them around you. Wow. But I haven't seem him since. Another guy flirted with me incessantly, then ignored me blatantly, then asked why I had changed. What? Maybe I'm not the only one with multiple personalities.

My friends tell me it's my fault. I'm not flirty enough or I should call him or he's crazy or greasy or self-absorbed or whatever. Maybe I still have a lot to learn. Maybe I have to go out with sixteen more guys before I meet someone who makes my cheeks hurt from smiling so much. Maybe I should go back to Wal-Mart and get some Mary Kate and Ashley Olsen lip gloss. Couldn't hurt, right?

I'm not defeated. I'm not done. Breaking up, in fact, didn't break me up. It really is true that what doesn't kill us makes us stronger.

Oh no.

Did I just say that?

THANKS

Of all the words, these are the hardest to write because there are so many who deserve so much. The following people saw me through at least one broken heart and merit much more than a small thanks. If you find your name listed here—I like you, I love you, I thank you. I am a rich, rich woman.

Jack and Ross—For breaking my heart. Otherwise I'd be forced to make this stuff up.

Mark Nicholas—For taking a chance on an unknown and an unfriendly. Your belief, insight, and friendship kept me from collapsing in a heap. And you take nice pictures, too.

AJ Fabulous Strout—For being fabulous and fantastic, for having an inner compass, being my stylist, my biggest fan, and my BFF in the thick of things. I wouldn't want to travel the world with anyone else.

Steve Strout—For helping with the hardest part.

Laura Perryman (Wan)—For reading and reading and reading and telling it like it is. And for living near Boston when I needed a friend.

Leigh Ann Scalf, Nivah Eckert, Laura Perryman, Beth Gallion and Ape Sanders—For being the kind of friends someone would write a chapter about. I do not deserve you.

Tiffany Leah Kelly—For space, colon, period . . . and so much more.

Heather Englert Davis—For AOT and all that . . .

My editors, Lori Jones and Kate Etue, and everyone at W Publishing Group—For thinking I might have something to say, and for helping me say it well.

Karina Bissinger—For living a life that belongs in a book. For giving me tulips and "amens" right when I needed them. And for the exact right mix of solitude and conversation.

My test subject, Joni Autrey—For being creative and genuine—and loving the early drafts enough to highlight!

Kim Nehs—For being classy. And for loving French fries as much as I do.

Costa Balamatsias—For designing a glamorous Web site.

Jen Pecinis—For being the booking agent of my dreams.

Thanks

My Internet Fan Base (who all promised to buy multiple copies)—For believing my long-winded speeches could some-day end up in a book.

My Flicker Family—For rock-'n'-roll.

Ladies of the House—For putting up with a moody writer who doubts daily.

Kellie Jane Soon-to-Be Harris—For saying yes to my brother. I love you already.

My Mom, Betty Harris—For being beautiful and talented and creative and witty and loved. I want to be like you when I grow up.

My Dad, Kelley Harris—For showing me what it means to love Jesus more than anything, just by the way you live your life.

Drew Harris—For being more than a brother and more than a friend. My life is richer because you love me.

Jesus—For being greater than my heart. For true love without condition. For being complete so that I don't have to be.

ABOUT **THE AUTHOR**

JoAnna Harris is a twenty-something from the South who lives in Nashville, Tennessee. Her days are spent at Flicker Records overseeing the sales of Christian rock bands like Pillar, Everyday Sunday, and The Swift. Her nights are filled writing, drinking Diet Coke, and practicing the art of being glamorous. She is a minor Internet celebrity with a devout following who periodically read her stories about losing love and then finding it again, but this is the first time her thoughts have been published for all to see.

JoAnna received her higher education at Union University with a degree in French, but speaks English when sharing God's sufficient grace with other women. She has experienced her fair share of heartbreak and relational upheaval, but in the end, found real Love and healing firsthand.

To learn more about JoAnna, visit
www.joannaharris.com.

To have JoAnna speak at your church or event, visit
www.joannaharris.com.

To e-mail JoAnna, visit
www.joannaharris.com.

To . . . well, why don't you just go ahead and visit
www.joannaharris.com.